DESIGNING SOUND
FOR ANIMATION

DESIGNING SOUND
FOR ANIMATION

2ND EDITION

ROBIN BEAUCHAMP

CRC Press
Taylor & Francis Group
Boca Raton London New York

CRC Press is an imprint of the
Taylor & Francis Group, an **informa** business

CRC Press
Taylor & Francis Group
6000 Broken Sound Parkway NW, Suite 300
Boca Raton, FL 33487-2742

First issued in hardback 2017

© 2013 by Taylor and Francis Group, LLC
CRC Press is an imprint of Taylor & Francis Group, an Informa business

ISBN-13: 978-0-240-82498-7 (pbk)
ISBN-13: 978-1-138-42854-6 (hbk)

Library of Congress Cataloging in Publication Data
Beauchamp, Robin.
    Designing sound for animation / Robin Beauchamp. — 2nd ed.
        p. cm.
    Includes bibliographical references and index.
    1. Sound motion pictures. 2. Sound—Recording and reproducing. 3. Animation (Cinematography) I. Title.
    TR897.B42 2013
    777'.53—dc23   2012019646

Typeset in Rotis
By Keystroke, Station Road, Codsall, Wolverhampton

Visit the Taylor & Francis Web site at
http://www.taylorandfrancis.com

and the CRC Press Web site at
http://www.crcpress.com

DEDICATION

To Leigh, Scott, Tyler, and Boomer

CONTENTS

LIST OF FIGURES AND TABLES

FIGURES

TABLES

THE AUTHOR

Robin Beauchamp is a professor of sound design at the Savannah College of Art and Design. There he teaches courses in sound design, music editing and supervision, ADR and Foley, and mixing. He is expert certified in Pro Tools Post Production and teaches certification courses in this area. Mr. Beauchamp continues to work as a music editor and sound designer for independent animations. The author may be contacted by email at rbeaucha@scad.edu.

CREDITS

ACKNOWLEDGMENTS

TECHNICAL READERS

Rob Miller, Steven LeGrand, Peter Damski, B.J. Sears, Matt Akers

POST PRODUCTION ADVISORS

David Stone, John Sisti, Vanessa Ament, Dane Davis, Gary Rydstrom, Paul and Angela Hackner

ANIMATION TECHNIQUE AND WORKFLOW

Joe Pasquale, John Webber, Jason Maurer, Hal Miles

ONLINE CONTENT

Alex Chabot, Dan Norton, Eric Williams

LEGAL

Debra Wagnon, Ernie Lee, Janice Shipp, Carmine Stowers

TECHNOLOGIES

Rob Campbell, Andy Cook, Avid; Thom Coach Ehle, Dolby Laboratories; Ron Ferrell, Phil Morales, Matt Harchic, Rich Rouleau, Lewis Herrin, Sean Redman, Michael Phipps; SCAD

LIBRARY MUSIC AND SFX

Marcie Jacobs, DeWolfe Music

Special thanks to the administration of the Savannah College of Art and Design for their support for this book: Paula Wallace (president), Brian Murphy (executive vice president and chief operating officer), Peter Weishar (dean of film and digital media).

To Tom Fischer and Pierre Archenbault, thank you for giving me the opportunity to teach and practice sound design.

To Chuck Lauter, for insisting that we all learn to write.

INTRODUCTION

OVERVIEW

The digital age has provided the independent animator possessing even modest resources access to the means to realize their creative visions. Academic programs have emerged to meet the growing interest in formal instruction in this art form. Those responsible for curriculum development face the daunting task of compressing essential animation courses into a traditional four-year program of study. Due to competing forces and limited resources, courses addressing soundtrack development are often under-represented. Consequently, there are gaps relating to soundtrack aesthetic and workflow that can potentially impede the independent animators ability to collaborate effectively. This book seeks to bridge this gap and assist the animator and sound design team in collaborative storytelling.

Methodology is not a substitute for personal logic.

Ronald B. Thomas

THE ELEMENTS OF A SOUNDTRACK

As you listen to the opening scene in Pixar's *Toy Story* (1995), notice the detail in which Andy intuitively adds sound to accompany his playtime. A diverse cast seamlessly toggles from character to character, each with their own readily identifiable voice. Filling the gaps between individual lines of dialogue are voiced sound effects that enhance the fantasy of the narrative being played out. This depiction of a child at play demonstrates that we learn, at a very early age, concepts that are fundamental to effective soundtrack development. As we mature, the ability to approach story telling with the same playful and creative ear remains essential. The three components of a soundtrack are dialogue, sound effects (SFX), and music. Sound designers and editors, directed by a supervising sound editor, create the dialogue and sound effects stems. A composer, music editor, and music supervisor develop the score separately. Re-recording mixers complete the soundtrack by blending

Every child is an artist. The problem is how to remain an artist once he grows up.

Pablo Picasso

all three elements at the final mix and preparing them for a variety of release formats. *Sound design* is a term that is often used to denote persons responsible for developing the sound effects and dialogue stems of the soundtrack. Though the term is typically reserved for SFX and dialogue, for the purpose of this text, we will from time to time use the term to include those persons responsible for the musical score as well.

SCOPE OF BOOK

The majority of writings on sound for image focus on live action, making only brief mention of the unique design considerations associated with animation. For example, the animation soundtrack is not tied to *production audio* (sound acquired on a live set) and must be completely constructed. In addition, there is a greater emphasis on the *animatic* (moving storyboard) created in pre-production, providing a working model by which initial components of the soundtrack can be developed. As with any collaborative effort, each participant must develop a working understanding of the aesthetics, tools, and workflow associated with aspects of the production; consequently, this book must serve multiple audiences: the animator, the sound designer, and the music department. At times, the animator might feel overwhelmed with the technical aspects of this book while the sound designer may feel a need for greater depth. A conscious decision was made to consider the needs of the animator first. The bibliography contains many of the significant writings on sound design to date for those seeking greater depth.

USING THIS BOOK

This book is designed as either a classroom text or self-directed study on soundtrack development for narrative short-form animation. Though the title, when taken literally, suggests a limited scope of 2D and 3D animation, many of the concepts presented apply equally to video games, web delivery, and live action film. Chapters 1 and 2 cover the foundations and theories of sound as they apply to audio/visual storytelling. The concepts addressed in these chapters provide a basic foundation in physics, acoustics, human perception, theory, and aesthetics. The vocabulary presented in these chapters will become more relevant as the reader works through the book and begins collaborating with the sound and music departments. The math has been simplified, the techno babble has been removed, and the acronyms have been spelled out, in the hope of closing the gap between conceptualization and application. Chapters 3 through 6 define the primary components or stems used in animation: dialogue, music, and sound effects. Each chapter explores the unique potential that individual stems contribute to the art of storytelling. Chapters 7 through 9 explore the production arc from the preproduction to layback. Chapter 10 contains references to a variety of feature length animations. These annotated references are designed to contextualize the concepts discussed throughout the book and guide your future listening efforts.

ABOUT THE 2ND EDITION

Few words resonate more with sound designers than Ben Burtt's quote regarding films escaping. His statement rings equally true for animators, composers, and authors. For most of us, there is rarely a second chance to revise our work once it has been screened or published. It is with this understanding that I wish to express my appreciation to Focal Press and the many readers for giving me the opportunity to create a 2nd edition. It is an honor to pull together the creative ideas and techniques of my colleagues, creating a book that represents their many contributions to the art of sound design and scoring. I appreciate the patience of the many professionals who have gently guided me toward accuracy in my attempt to bridge professional practice with academic delivery. I sincerely hope that this text will assist aspiring animators and sound designers in the collaborative effort to produce a soundtrack that "escapes" with style.

> Films are never released, they just escape.
>
> Ben Burtt

ONLINE CONTENT

Online delivery provides a seamless bridge between the written word and other forms of media. The second edition of *Designing Sound for Animation* comes with a full complement of online materials including four films, each presented as a full mix or as isolated stems. Also included in the online content area is a sound design kit containing the film *Pasttime* and a folder of sounds that can be used to re-create the soundtrack. This kit is intended to provide a hands-on experience with many of the concepts and techniques addressed in the book. Feel free to use these sounds or to substitute them with your personal library. Additional QuickTime movies have been provided to further explain some of the more abstract concepts covered in Chapter 1.

Many of the illustrations and photos presented throughout the text are also available for download as high resolution, resizable, color .tif files. Finally, a test bank has been created for each chapter to assist instructors who use this text to complement their courses.

FOUNDATIONS OF AUDIO FOR IMAGE

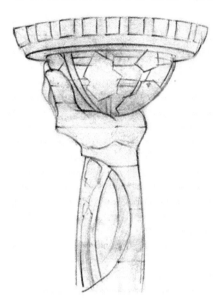

OVERVIEW

The concepts presented in this chapter are intended to develop conceptual common ground and a working vocabulary that facilitates communication between the filmmaker, sound designer, and composer. Where possible, these concepts are presented in the context of the narrative film.

PERCEPTION OF SOUND

SOUND

There are three basic requirements for sound to exist in the physical world. First, there must be a *sound source*, such as a gunshot, which generates acoustic energy. The acoustic energy must then be transmitted through a *medium* such as air. Finally, a *receiver*, such as a listener's ears, must perceive and interpret this acoustic energy as *sound*. In Film, the animator creates the first two conditions, the sound designer represents these conditions with sound, and the audience processes the sound to derive meaning. Sound can also be experienced as a part of our thoughts, in a psychological process known as *audiation.* As you are silently reading this book, the words are sounding in your head. Just as animators visualize their creations, composers and sound designers conceptualize elements of the soundtrack through the process of audiation. Voice over (in the first person) allows us to hear the interior thoughts of a character, an example of scripted audiation.

> Audio without image is called radio, video without audio is called surveillance.
>
> Anonymous

> To listen is an effort, and just to hear is no merit. A duck hears also.
>
> Igor Stravinsky

HEARING VERSUS LISTENING

When acoustic energy arrives at our ears, it excites the hearing apparatus and causes a physiological sensation, interpreted by the brain as sound. This physiological process is called *hearing*. However, if we are to derive meaning from sound, we must first perceive and respond to the sound through active *listening*. Audiences can actively listen to a limited number of sounds present in the soundtrack. Fortunately, they can also filter extraneous sounds while focusing on selected sounds; this phenomenon is known as the *cocktail effect*. One shared goal of sound design and mixing is to focus the audience's attention on specific sounds critical to the narrative.

LOCALIZATION

In most theaters (and an increasing number of homes), sound extends beyond the screen to include the sides and back of the room. The physical space implied by this speaker configuration is referred to as the *sound field*. Our ability to perceive specific sound placements within this field is known as *localization* (Figure 1.1).

The panners (pan pots) on a mixing board facilitate the movement of sound from left to right by adjusting the relative levels presented in each speaker. Using this approach, individual sounds can be placed (*panned*) within the sound field to accurately match on-screen visuals even as they move.

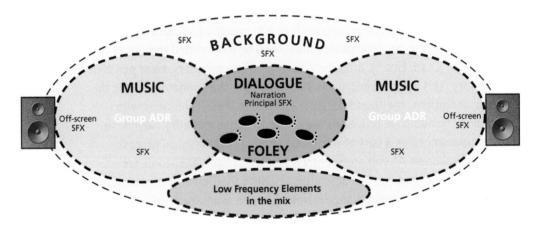

Figure 1.1 The Soundtrack in the Sound Field

Off-screen action can be implied by panning sound to the far left or right in the stereo field (Figure 1.2).

Independent film submission requirements typically call for a stereo mix but there is an increasing acceptance of multi-channel mixes. *Multi-channel* sound extends the sound field behind the audience (surrounds). The surrounds have been used primarily to deliver ambient sounds but this role is expanding with the popularity of stereoscopic (3D) films. Walt Disney pioneered multi-channel mixing with the Fanta-sound presentations of "Fantasia" in the late 1930s, adding height perspective for the sixtieth anniversary screening.

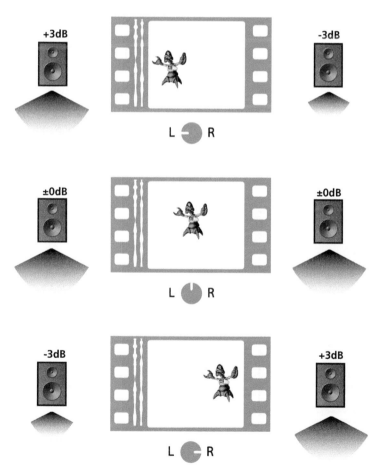

Figure 1.2 Volume Panning

ACOUSTICS

Acoustics is a term associated with the characteristics of sound interacting in a given space. Film mixers apply reverb and delay to the soundtrack to establish and reinforce the space implied onscreen. The controls or parameters of these processors can be used to establish the size and physical properties of a space as well as relative distances between objects. One of the most basic presets on a reverb plug-in is the reverb type or room (Figure 1.3).

The terms *dry* and *wet* are subjective terms denoting direct and reflected sound. Re-recording mixers frequently adjust the reverb settings to support transitions from environment to environment.

RHYTHM AND TEMPO

Rhythm is the identifiable pattern of sound and silence. The speed of these patterns is referred to as the *tempo*. Tempo can remain constant to provide continuity, or accelerate/decelerate to match the visual timings of on-screen images. Footsteps, clocks, and heartbeats are all examples of sound objects that typically have recognizable rhythm and tempo. Vehicles, weapons, and dialogue are often varied in this respect. Many sounds such as footsteps or individual lines of dialogue derive additional meaning from the rhythm and

Figure 1.3 Reverb Room Presets

tempo of their delivery. This is an important point to consider when editing sound to picture. Composers often seek to identify the rhythm or pacing of a scene when developing the rhythmic character of their cues.

NOISE AND SILENCE

The aesthetic definition of *noise* includes any unwanted sound found in the soundtrack. Noise always exists to some degree and sound editors and mixers have many tools and techniques to minimize noise. Backgrounds are sometimes mistakenly referred to as noise. However, backgrounds are carefully constructed to add depth to a scene whereas noise is carefully managed as not to detract from the narrative. *Silence* is perhaps the least understood component of sound design. Silence can be an effective means of creating tension, release, or contrast. However, complete silence is unnatural and can pull the audience out of the narrative. Silence before an explosion creates contrast, effectively making the explosion perceptually louder.

> It's the space between the notes that give them meaning.
>
> Nathan East

THE PHYSICS OF SOUND

SOUND WAVES

The sine wave is the most basic component of sound. The horizontal line shown in Figure 1.4 represents the *null or zero point*, the point at which no

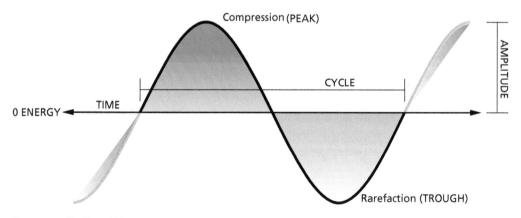

Figure 1.4 *The Sound Wave*

energy exists. The space above the line represents high pressure (*compression*) that pushes inward on our hearing mechanisms. The higher the wave ascends, the greater the sound pressure, the more volume we perceive. The highest point in the excursion above the line is the *peak*. The space below the line represents low pressure (*rarefaction*). As the wave descends, a vacuum is created which pulls outward on our hearing mechanism. The lowest point in the downward excursion is the *trough*. A single, 360° excursion of a wave (over time) is a *cycle*.

FREQUENCY

Frequency, determined by counting the number of *cycles* per second, is expressed in units called *hertz* (Hz); one cycle per second is equivalent to 1 hertz (Figure 1.5).

Pitch is our subjective interpretation of *frequency* such as the tuning note for an orchestra being A=440 Hertz. The *frequency* range for humans begins on average at 20 Hz and extends upwards of 20,000 Hz (20 kHz). *Frequency response* refers to the range of fundamental frequencies that an object can produce. Frequency response is a critical factor in the selection of microphones, recording devices, headphones, speakers, and commercial SFX/Music. It is also an important qualitative feature relating to audio compression codecs such as Mp3 and AAC. In musical terms, the frequency range of human hearing is 10 octaves, eight of which are present in a grand piano (Figure 1.6).

Frequency can be used to re-enforce many narrative principles such as age, size, gender, and speed. SFX are often pitched up or down to create contrast or to work harmoniously with the score. There are physiological relationships between frequency and human perception that can be used to enhance the cinematic experience. For example, low frequencies travel up our bodies through our feet,

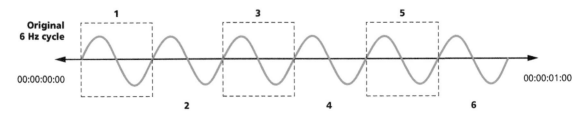

Figure 1.5 Six Cycles Per Second

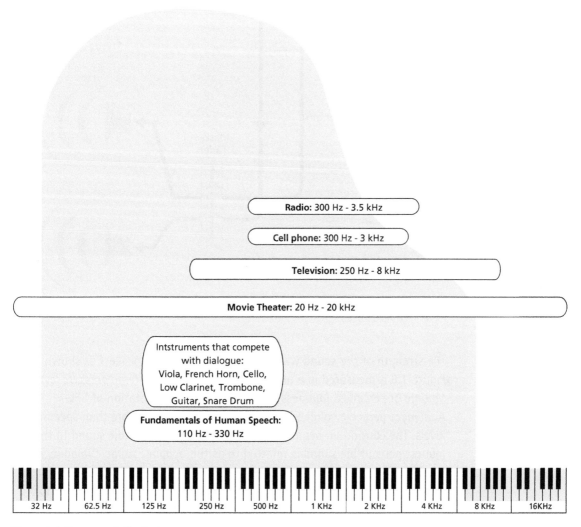

Radio: 300 Hz - 3.5 kHz

Cell phone: 300 Hz - 3 kHz

Television: 250 Hz - 8 kHz

Movie Theater: 20 Hz - 20 kHz

Intstruments that compete
with dialogue:
Viola, French Horn, Cello,
Low Clarinet, Trombone,
Guitar, Snare Drum

Fundamentals of Human Speech:
110 Hz - 330 Hz

32 Hz | 62.5 Hz | 125 Hz | 250 Hz | 500 Hz | 1 KHz | 2 KHz | 4 KHz | 8 KHz | 16KHz

Figure 1.6 Frequency in Context

creating a vertical sensation. Consequently low frequency content can be
brought up or down in the mix to enhance visuals that move vertically.

AMPLITUDE

When acoustic energy is digitized, the resultant wave is referred to as a
signal. Amplitude is used to describe the amount of energy (voltage) present
in the signal (Figure 1.7).

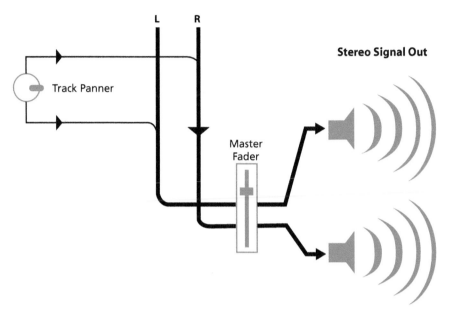

Figure 1.7 Amplitude

The strength of the sound waves emanating from the speakers as shown in Figure 1.6 is measured in a unit called *dB SPL (decibel sound pressure level)*. *Volume* or perceived *loudness* is our subjective interpretation of SPL. Audiences perceive volume in terms of relative change more than specific dB levels. The continuum beginning from the softest perceptible sound to the loudest perceptible sound is referred to as the *dynamic range*. Dialogue, if present, is the most important reference used by audiences to judge the volume levels for playback. Re-recording mixers use amplitude or level to create intensity, provide emphasis, promote scale or size, and establish proximity of sound objects. An audience's perception of volume is also linked with frequency. Human hearing is most sensitive in the mid-range frequencies. More amplitude is required for low and high frequencies to match the apparent loudness of the mid-range frequencies. This perceptual curve is known as the *equal loudness curve*. This curve influences how we mix and why we seek to match the playback levels on the mix stage with the playback levels in theaters *(reference level)*.

TIMBRE

The combination of a fundamental frequency and associated harmonics combine to create a unique aural signature that we refer to as *timbre* or *tone quality*. We have the ability to discretely identify objects or characters solely by timbre. Composers select instruments to play specific components of a cue based largely on timbre. Timbre plays an important role in voice casting, the selection of props for Foley, and nearly every SFX developed for the soundtrack (Figure 1.8).

WAVELENGTH

Wavelength is the horizontal measurement of the complete cycle of a wave. Wavelengths are inversely proportionate to frequency and low frequencies can be up to 56 feet in length. The average ear span of an adult is approximately 7 inches. Waves of varied length interact uniquely with this fixed ear span. Low-frequency waves are so large that they wrap around our ears and reduce our ability to determine the direction (*localization*) of the sound source. The closer the length of a wave is to our ear span (approx 2 kHz), the easier it is for us to localize. One popular application of this

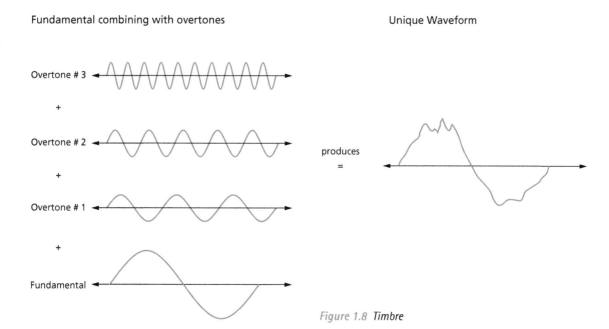

Figure 1.8 *Timbre*

concept is the use of low-frequency sound effects to rouse our "fight or flight" response. When audiences are presented with visual and sonic stimuli determined to be dangerous, the body instinctively prepares to fight or escape. If the audience cannot determine the origin or direction of the sound because the sounds are low in frequency, their sense of fear and vulnerability is heightened.

SPEED OF SOUND

Sound travels at roughly 1130 feet per second through air at a temperature of 70°F; the more dense the medium (steel *versus* air), the faster the sound travels. The speed of sound is equal at all frequencies. In reality, light travels significantly faster than sound. Therefore, we see an action or object before we hear it; however, the cinematic practice for sound editing is to sync the audio on or slightly after the action; this is referred to as *hard sync*.

DIGITAL AUDIO

DIGITIZING AUDIO

Digital audio has impacted nearly every aspect of soundtrack production. When handled properly, digital audio can be copied and manipulated with minimal degradation to the original sound file. Digital audio is not without its drawbacks, however, and it is important to understand its basic characteristics in order to preserve the quality of the signal. The conversion of acoustic energy to digital audio is most commonly achieved in a process known as LPCM or Linear Pulse Code Modulation. An analog signal is digitized using specialized computer chips known as analog-to-digital (A/D) converters. A/D converters are designed to deliver a range of audio resolutions by sampling a range of frequencies at discrete amplitudes. D/A converters reverse this process to deliver analog signals for playback. The quality of A/D converters vary from device to device and are often a factor in the cost of higher end audio equipment (Figure 1.9).

SAMPLING RATES

The visual component of animation is represented by a minimum of 24 frames per second. As the frame rate dips below this visual threshold,

A/D Conversion

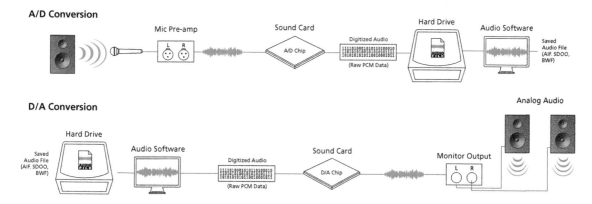

D/A Conversion

Figure 1.9 A/D Conversion

the image begins to flicker (persistence of vision). Similar thresholds exist for digital audio as well. Frequency is captured digitally by sampling at more than twice the rate of the highest frequency present, referred to as the *Nyquist frequency* (Figure 1.10).

If the sampling rate falls below this frequency, the resultant audio will become filled with frequencies that were not present in the original

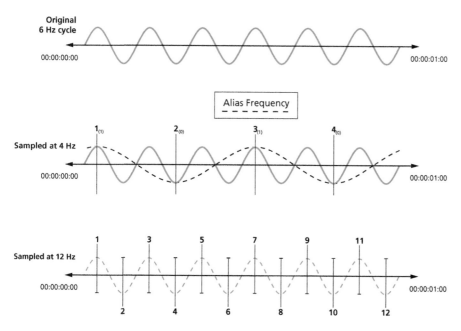

Figure 1.10 Nyquist Frequency

(harmonic distortion). The minimum sampling rate for film and television is 48 kHz with high definition video sample rates extending up to 192 kHz. The sampling rates of web delivery are often lower than the NTSC standard. The process of converting from a higher sample rate to a lower sample rate is referred to as *down sampling.*

BIT-DEPTHS

The amplitude of a wave is captured by sampling the energy of a wave at various points over time and assigning each point a value in terms of voltage. *Bit-depth* refers to the increments or resolution used to describe amplitude. At a bit-depth of two, the energy of a wave is sampled in four equal increments (Figure 1.11).

Notice that all portions of the wave between the sampling increments are rounded up or down (quantized) to the nearest value. *Quantization* produces errors (noise) that are sonically equivalent to visual pixilation. As the bit-depth is increased, the resolution improves and the resulting signal looks and sounds more analogous to the original (Figure 1.12).

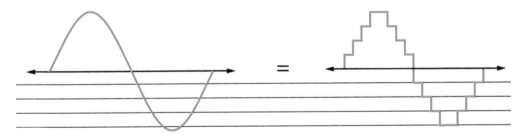

Figure 1.11 *Low Bit-Depth Resolution*

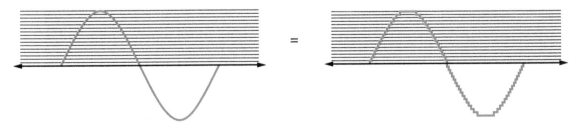

Figure 1.12 *High Bit-Depth Resolution*

In theoretical terms, each added bit increases the dynamic range by 6.01 dB (16 bit = 96 dB). The professional delivery standard for film and television soundtracks is currently 16 to 24 bit. However, sound editors often work at bit depths up to 32 bit when performing amplitude based signal processing. The process of going from a higher bit depth to a lower bit depth is called *dither*.

AUDIO COMPRESSION

PCM (pulse code modulation) is a non-compressed or full resolution digital audio file. Non-compressed audio represents the highest quality available for media production. File extensions such as aiff, .wav, and BWF are added to a PCM file to make them readable by computers. In a perfect world, all audio for media would be full resolution. However, due to file storage and transfer limitations for Internet, package media, and broadcast formats, audio compression continues to be a practical reality. Audio codecs (compression/decompression) have been developed to meet delivery requirements for various release formats. Of these, the most common are mp3, AAC, AC-3, and DTS. The available settings on a codec have a direct impact on the frequency response of the resultant files. For example, higher transfer rates preserve more of the high frequency content in the original file. Therefore, it is important to know the allowable transfer rate and file size limitations for specific release formats when encoding the audio. For Internet delivery, streaming options are typically lower than download options. Though the differences between high and low resolution audio may not be readily heard on consumer monitors or head phones, these differences are dramatic when played through high quality speakers like those found in theaters. Therefore it is important to understand what type of monitors your potential audiences will be listening to and compress accordingly.

CHAPTER 2

SOUND DESIGN THEORY

OVERVIEW

The pairing of audio and visual media is part of our everyday experiences. Armed with an ipod and earbuds, we intuitively underscore our daily commutes and recreation time through carefully selected song-lists. We visualize while listening to the radio and we audiate while reading. In the absence of either sound or picture, audiences will create that which is not present, potentially redefining the original intention of any given work. Therefore, in narrative animation, we must carefully select the content used in this pairing as we guide the audience through the story. To accomplish this, we must first understand the unique relationship of sound paired with image. As early as 1928 with the release of *Steamboat Willie*, directors, editors, and composers have explored this relationship as they develop the aesthetic for creative sound design.

No theory is good except on condition that one use it to go beyond.

Andre Gide

SOUND CLASSIFICATIONS

CHION CLASSIFICATIONS

Michel Chion (a noted sound theorist) classifies listening in three modes: causal, semantic, and reduced. Chion's typology provides a useful design framework for discussing sounds function in a soundtrack. *Causal* sound is aptly named, as it reinforces cause and effect (see a cow, hear a cow). Sound editors often refer to these as *hard effects*, especially when they are used in a literal fashion. The saying "we don't have to see everything we hear, but we need to hear most of what we see" describes the practical role that causal sounds play in the soundtrack. The term *semantic* is used to categorize sound in which literal meaning is the primary emphasis. Speech, whether in a native or foreign tongue, is a form of semantic sound. Morse code is also semantic and, like foreign languages, requires a mechanism for translation (e.g.

Figure 2.1 *The Footsteps for the Fire Extinguisher Are Covered with the Non-Literal Sound of a Spray Paint Can Being Shaken in the Film* Mercury Inspection *(2006), Directed by Leslie Wisley Padien*

They forgot to turn off the ambience again!–

Alex (*Madagascar*)

subtitles) when used to deliver story points. Even the beeps placed over curse words imply a semantic message. The term *reduced* refers to sounds that are broken down, or reduced, to their fundamental elements and paired with new objects to create new meanings. Animation provides many opportunities for this non-literal use of sound.

DIEGETIC AND NON-DIEGETIC SOUND

The term *diegetic* denotes sound that is perceived by the characters in the film. Though unbeknownst to the characters, diegetic sound is also perceived by the audience. This use of sound establishes a voyeuristic relationship between the characters and their audience. *Non-diegetic* sound is heard exclusively by the audience, often providing them with more information than is provided to the characters. When discussing music cues, the terms *source* and *underscore* are used in place of diegetic and non-diegetic. Diegetic sound promotes the implied reality of a scene. Principle dialogue, hard effects, and source music are all examples of diegetic sound. In contrast, non-diegetic components of a soundtrack promote a sense of fantasy. Examples of non-diegetic sound include narration, laugh tracks, and underscore. The cinematic boundaries of diegesis are often broken or combined to meet the narrative intent at any given moment.

NARRATIVE FUNCTIONS

GUIDED PERCEPTION

If that squeak sounds kind of sad and you never meant it to sound sad, it will throw it that way, so you can't ignore it.–

Andrew Stanton

The images presented within a scene are often ambiguous in nature, inviting the audience to search for non-visual clues as they attempt to clarify both meaning and intensity. Within these shots are creative opportunities to guide the audience perceptually from frame to frame. The editors and composers for the early Warner and MGM shorts understood this and became masters at guiding the audience's perception. They accomplished this by using non-literal sound for subjective scenes. Disney also uses this design approach when producing films for younger audiences. For example, in *Beauty and the*

Beast, the final conflict between the villagers and the castle's servants is underscored with a playful rendition of "Be our Guest". Here, the score guides the audience to a non-literal interpretation of the visuals, promoting a "softer" perception of the content, thus making the film appropriate to a wider audience.

DRAWING THE AUDIENCE INTO THE NARRATIVE

The title sequence is typically the first opportunity for soundtrack to contribute to the storytelling process. Like a hypnotist, the sound design team and composer develop elements for the title sequence to draw the audience out of their present reality and into the cinematic experience. Sound designers and re-recording mixers take great care to keep the audience in the narrative. At the conclusion of the film, the soundtrack can provide closure while transitioning the audience back to their own reality.

DIRECTING THE EYE

Re-recording mixers create sonic foregrounds, mid-grounds, and backgrounds using volume, panning, delay, and reverb. They choose what the audience hears and the perspective for which it is heard. Subtle visuals can be brought into focus with carefully placed audio that directs the eye (Figure 2.2).

Cocktail Tray	Synchronized Sound	Guided Perception
	Sonar Ping	Directing our attention to the submerged olive.
	Song "Auld Lang Syne"	Establishing the season and emotional tone.
	Ambulance Siren	Forshadowing cause and effect.

Figure 2.2 The Picture Displays a Martini Glass, an Ashtray, and a Wine Bottle. By Pairing a Seemingly Unrelated Sonar Ping with this Frame, Audiences Are Challenged to Find a Relationship or Gestalt between the Two, the Desired Effect Being that the Eyes are Directed to the Submerged Olive

ESTABLISHING OR CLARIFYING POINT OF VIEW

In a scene from *Ratatouille* (2007), Remy and Emile (rats) are being chased by an elderly French woman in her kitchen. When we experience the scene through their perspective, the principle dialogue is spoken in English. However, when the perspective shifts to the elderly women, their dialogue is reduced to rat-like squeaks. This is an example of dialogue effectively transitioning with the point of view (POV) within a scene. In *Toy Story* (1995), Gary Rydstrom (sound designer) and Randy Newman (composer) contrast diegetic sound and underscore in a street-crossing scene. The world as heard from the perspective of the toys is primarily musical. In contrast, distance shots of the toys are covered with hard effects and BGs. Cinema has borrowed a technique from Opera where specific thematic music is assigned to individual characters. This approach to scoring is referred to as *Leitmotif* and is often used to establish or clarify the POV of a scene, especially where more than one character is present. Sound designers often pitch shift or harmonize props in an attempt to create a sonic distinction between characters.

CLARIFYING THE SUBTEXT

> You have to find some way of saying it without saying it.
>
> Duke Ellington

During the silent film era, actors were prone to exaggerated expressions or gestures to convey the emotion of a scene. With the arrival of synchronized sound, the actor was liberated from exaggerated acting techniques. When a character is animated with a neutral or ambiguous expression, an opportunity for the soundtrack to reveal the characters' inner thoughts or feelings is created. When a music cue is written specifically to clarify the emotion of the scene, it is referred to as *subtext scoring*. Subtext scoring is more immediate and specific than dialogue at conveying the emotion. The subtext can also be clarified through specific design elements or BGs.

CONTRASTING REALITY AND SUBJECTIVITY

Though animation is subjective by nature, there exists an implied reality that can be contrasted with subjective moments such as slow motion scenes, montage sequences, and dream sequences. Subjective moments are often reinforced sonically by means of contrast. One common design approach to subjective moments is to minimize or remove all diegetic sound. This approach is often used in montage sequences where music is often the exclusive sound driving the sequence. In slow motion sequences, diegetic sound is typically slowed down and lowered in pitch to simulate analog tape effects. Though clichéd in approach, dream sequences are often reinforced with additional reverb to distance the sound from reality.

EXTENDING THE FIELD OF VISION

There is a saying that a picture is worth a thousand words. In radio (theater of the mind), sound is worth a thousand pictures. When objects producing sound are visible, the sound is referred to as *sync sound* or *on-screen*. *Off-screen* sound can introduce and follow objects as they move on and off-screen, thereby re-enforcing the visual line established through a series of shots. Our field of vision is limited to roughly 180°, requiring visual cuts and camera movements to overcome this limitation. Multi-channel soundtracks, on the other hand, are omni-directional and can be used to extend the boundaries of a shot beyond the reach of the eye. The classic *camera shake* used by Hanna-Barbera is a visual approach to storytelling where off-screen sound is used to imply that which is not shown. This approach serves to minimize the perceived intensity of the impacts while avoiding costly and time-consuming animation. Multi-channel mixing has the potential to mirror front-to-back movements while extending the depth of a scene to include the space behind the audience. With the growing use of stereoscopic projection, there is increased potential for multi-channel mixing to mirror the movement of 3-dimensional images.

> The ears are the guardians of our sleep.
>
> Randy Thom

TENSION AND RELEASE

Tension and release is a primary force in all art forms. Film composers have many means of creating tension, such as the shock chords (dissonant clusters of notes) featured prominently in the early animations of Warner Brother and MGM studios. Another approach common to this period was the harmonization of a melody with minor 2nds. The suspension or resolution of a tonal chord progression or the lack of predictability in atonal harmonic motion can produce wide ranges of tension and release. A *build* is a cue that combines harmonic tension and volume to create an expectation for a given event. Some sounds have inherent qualities that generate tension or release and are often used metaphorically. For example, air-raid sirens, crying babies, emergency vehicles, growling animals, and snake rattles all evoke tension.

Conversely, the sound of crickets, lapping waves, and gentle rain produce a calming effect. Either type of sound can be used directly or blended (*sweetened)* with literal sounds to create a subliminal effect on the audience.

CONTINUITY

> I was looking for a special sound and it was kind of keyed into the design of the movie.
>
> Brad Bird

Continuity has always been an important aesthetic in filmmaking, regardless of length. In a narrative animation, continuity is not a given; it must be constructed. For this reason, directors hire a supervising sound editor to insure that the dialogue and SFX are also cohesive. In Disney's *Treasure Planet* (2002), director Ron Clemons developed a 70/30 rule to guide the design for the production. The result was a visual look that featured a blending of eighteenth-century elements (70 percent) with modern elements (30 percent). Dane Davis, sound designer for *Treasure Planet*, applied this rule when designing SFX and dialogue to produce an "antique future" for this soundtrack. Continuity is not limited to the physical and temporal realms,

Figure 2.3 In the Film Painting Day *(2003) Directed by Daesup Chang, Elements of the Soundtrack Were Intentionally Limited to Those that Existed in the Old West*

emotional continuity is equally important. The score is often the key to emotional continuity. Perhaps this is why few scores are written by multiple composers. It takes great insight to get to the core of a character's feelings and motivations and even greater talent to express those aspects across the many cuts and scenes that make up a film. When developing cues, continuity can be promoted through instrumentation. For example, in *The Many Adventures of Winnie the Pooh* (1977), composer Buddy Baker assigned specific instruments to each of the characters.

PROMOTING CHARACTER DEVELOPMENT

An effective soundtrack helps us identify with the characters and their story. Animators create characters, not actors. Much of the acting occurs in the dialogue while SFX reinforce the character's physical traits and movements. The score is perhaps the most direct means of infusing a character with emotional qualities. Character development is not limited to people. In animation, virtually any object can be personified (*anthropomorphism*) through dialogue, music, and effects. Conversely, humans are often *caricatured* in animation. For example, the plodding footsteps of Fred Flintstone are often covered with a tuba or bassoon to emphasize his oversized physique and personality.

THEORETICAL CONCEPTS SPECIFIC TO DIALOGUE

Dialogue is processed in a different manner than SFX or music in that audiences are primarily focused on deriving meaning, both overt and concealed. Consequently, dialogue tracks do not require literal panning and are most often panned to the center. One notable exception to this practice can be heard in the 1995 film *Casper*, where the dialogue of the ghost characters pans around the room as only ghosts can. Narration, like underscore, is non-diegetic, promoting the narrative fantasy and requiring a greater willing suspension of disbelief. Narration is sometimes processed with additional reverb and panned in stereo, placing it in a different narrative space than principle dialogue. When Fred Flintstone speaks *direct to the camera*, he is breaking the sonic boundary (diegesis) that normally exists between the characters and the audience. This style of delivery is referred to as *breaking the 4th wall.* One clever application of both concepts is the introduction of principle dialogue off-screen, suggesting narration, and then through a series of shots, revealing the character speaking direct to camera. This allows dialogue to deliver story points while also minimizing animation for speech.

THEORETICAL CONCEPTS SPECIFIC TO SCORE

> You're trying to create a sonic landscape that these drawings can sit on . . . and these characters can live within.
>
> Hans Zimmer
> (The Lion King)

In addition to establishing the POV of a scene, an established *leitmotif* can allow audiences to experience the presence of a specific character, even when that character is off-screen. The abstract nature of animation often calls for a *metaphoric sound* treatment. For example, in *A Bug's Life* (1998), the back and forth movement of a bowed violin is used to exaggerate the scratching motion of a bug in a drunken state. The use of musical cues to mimic movement is known as *isomorphism*. Ascending/descending scales and pitch bending add directionality to isomorphism. The use of musical instruments as a substitution for hard effects gained favor in the early years of film as it facilitated coverage of complex visual action without requiring cumbersome sound editing. Percussion instruments in particular became a fast and effective means of representing complex rhythmic visuals. The substitution of musical intervals for Foley footsteps *(sneak steps)* began as early as 1929 with Disney's *The Skeleton Dance*. The melodic intervals and synchronized rhythm help to exaggerate the movement while specifying the emotional feel. *Anempathetic* cues are deliberately scored to contrast the implied emotion of a scene. This technique is typically used to increases an audience's empathy for the protagonists or to mock a character. *Misdirection* is a classic technique where the score builds toward a false conclusion. This technique is often used for dream sequences or as a setup for visual gags. Acoustic or synthetic instrumentation can be used to contrast organic and synthetic characters or environments. The size of instrumentation or orchestration establishes the scale of the film or the intimacy of a scene. Conversely, a full orchestra can give a scene an epic feel. Score can function transitionally as well. For example, a cue can morph from *source-to-underscore* as a scene transitions to a more subjective nature.

THEORETICAL CONCEPTS SPECIFIC TO SFX

> Sound effects are a huge part of making us believe in these characters and connect to them emotionally.
>
> Ethan Van Der Ryn

Sound effects are an effective means of establishing narrative elements such as time period, location, and character development. For example, seagulls imply the ocean, traffic implies urban settings, and machinery implies

Figure 2.4 An Acoustic Bass Covers the Individual Footsteps (Sneak Steps) in the Sandlot Fantasy Pasttime *(2004) Directed by Todd Hill*

industry. World War II air-raid sirens and steam-powered trains are historical icons that help to clarify the time period. Characters are often developed through associated props, such as a typewriter (journalist) or a whistle blast (traffic cop). Many sounds elicit emotional responses from an audience due to their *associative nature*. Sounds have the potential of revealing or clarifying the underlying meaning or subtext of a scene. For example, the pairing of a gavel with a cash register *(sweetening)* implies that justice is for sale. Visual similarities between two objects such as a ceiling fan and a helicopter blade can be re-enforced by morphing their respective sounds as the images transition, this is referred to as a *form edit* (Table 2.1). Sound effects are often used to de-emphasize the intensity of the visuals, especially when used to represent off-screen events and objects.

Table 2.1 Form Edits

Woodpecker (country)	Jackhammer (urban)
Flock of geese (organized activity)	Traffic jam (breakdown)
Alarm clock (internal)	Garbage truck backing up (external)
Telegraph (antique)	Fax machine (modern)
Typewriter (documentation)	Gunshot (flashback to event)

INTERPRETING PICTURE EDITS

OVERVIEW

In Hollywood there are no rules, but break them at your own peril.

Peter Guber

In the early years of film, picture editors handled many of the tasks now handled by sound editors. They intuitively understood how the picture editor directed the flow of images, established a rhythm, maintained continuity, and facilitated the narrative. They were also sensitive to the implications of camera angles, camera movement, and framing. As a result, their sound edits were visually informed. As sound design evolves into a more specialized field, it is important for sound editors to maintain this perspective. This can be a challenging proposition for when properly executed, picture editing is nearly transparent to the audience. Sound designers and composers must develop an awareness of visual cues and their implications for sound design. The purpose of this section is to establish a common language for both picture and sound editors. There is a danger when discussing this broad a topic in a shortened format. While reading the following, be mindful that the craft and creativity of editing cannot be reduced to a set of rigid rules. As you work on each film, allow that film to evolve by never allowing methodology to be a substitute for personal logic and feelings. No filmmaker ever hoped his audience would leave the theater saying "boy that was a well-edited film."

SHOTS

The most basic element of the film is the *frame*. A series of uninterrupted frames constitute a *shot* or, in editor language, a clip. A sequence of related shots are assembled to create a *scene*. Some shots are *cut* and digitally spliced while others are given a transitional treatment such as a *wipe* or *dissolve*. In most cases, the goal of picture and sound editing is to move from shot to shot with the greatest transparency. Storyboards, shot lists, and spotting sessions are all important means of communicating the vision of the film and the nuance associated with each frame, shot, and edit.

Framing

During the storyboard stage, the animator designs a series of shots to develop a scene. There is a multitude of approaches to individual shots and a wide range of verbiage to describe each. One aspect of the shot is *framing*, which establishes the distance of the audience from the subject. From close-up to extreme long shot, framing has its counterpart in the foreground and background of the soundtrack. For example, close-up shots (CU) isolate an action or expression, eliminating peripheral distractions. Therefore the soundtrack supports this perspective by minimizing off-screen sounds. Long shots, on the other hand, provide a more global perspective, and are better suited for sonic treatments of a more ambient nature. When designing sound for animation, it is important to consider individual shots in the larger context of a sequence. For example, in an action sequence, it is common to frame the same subject from many different perspectives. As a result, the movements of these objects appear to move faster or slower depending on the framing. To promote continuity, this type of sequence is often scored at a continuous tempo, creating a unified sense of pacing when played through the scene.

Camera Placement

Camera placements offer a variety of ways to portray a character. The most common camera placement is at the eye level. This placement implies a neutral or equal relationship with the subject. When the camera angle points up to a character, the intent often indicates a position of power. The reverse might also be true but it is important to clarify intent before designing sound based on camera placement alone. The *over-the-shoulder shot* blocks our view of the character's mouth, creating an opportunity to add or alter lines of dialogue in post-production. This placement also shifts the perspective to another character, often revealing that character's reaction to what is being said.

Camera Movement

Camera movements can be horizontal *(pan)*, vertical *(tilt)*, or move inward and outward *(zoom)*. Both pan and vertical shots are often motivated by the need to reveal more information in an extended environment. Pan shots are often underscored and/or designed with static backgrounds that provide continuity for the camera move. Tilt and zoom shots are more common in animation as they often promote an exaggerated feel. Isomorphic cues are commonly used to score these types of camera movements. A *pull back shot* gradually moves away from a subject to reveal a new environment. This type of shot can be supported by morphing from one set of BGs to another or by opening up the sound field in the mix. Though not a camera move, the shift of camera focus from the foreground to the background, known as *pulling focus*, is a natural transition within a scene. The re-recording mixer can mirror this transition by shifting elements of the soundtrack from the sonic background to the sonic foreground.

Movement of Objects

Fly-bys and *fly-throughs* refer to objects moving in relationship to a fixed camera position to create the illusion that an object is passing left to right or front to back. Fly-bys are re-enforced by panning sound left or right as indicated by the on-screen movement. Fly-throughs can be realized by panning to and from the screen channels and the surround channels as indicated by the on-screen movement. When panning bys of either type, it is still important to observe the line. Processing the sound object with Doppler and/or adding *whoosh effects* can provide additional motion and energy to the visual by. Doppler is the dynamic change of pitch and volume of an object as it approaches and passes by the audience.

Perspective Shot (POV)

In a *perspective (POV) shot* we experience the action subjectively through the eyes of a specific character. Just as we are seeing with their eyes, so too are we hearing through their ears. A good example of POV can be heard in *The Ant Bully* (2006), where the audience views the action through the mask of a bug exterminator. This perspective was achieved by contrasting the exterminator's breathing (interior) with the muffled sound of the environment (exterior).

Insert Shots and Cutaways

An *insert shot* cuts from a shot framed at a greater distance to close-up shot. Insert shots are used to reveal detailed information like the time on a watch or a message written on a note. The insert shot can be further exaggerated by briefly suspending the time of the reveal by *freezing the frame*. One effective design approach to freeze-frames is to cut the SFX and dialogue (diegetic elements) but play the underscore (non-diegetic and linear). A *cutaway shot* moves to a framing of greater distance, providing information from larger objects like a grandfather clock or a billboard sign. Sound elements that hit with a reveal are typically timed a few frames late to suggest the character's reaction time. If the soundtrack does not hit when the information is revealed, it is said to *play through the scene*. In the early years of animation, music cues hit on much of the action, a technique referred to as *Mickey Mousing*. This technique is used more sparingly today and many directors view its use in a negative context. However, in the hands of a skilled composer, cues can hit a significant portion of the action without calling attention to the technique.

CUTS

A *cut* is the most common type of edit and consists of two shots joined without any transitional treatment. In Walter Murch's book *In the Blink of an Eye* (2001), Murch discusses the cut as a cinematic experience unique to visual media and dreams. As part of our "willing suspension of disbelief," audiences have come to accept cuts as a normal part of the film experience. Sound editors often use the terms *audio clip* and *audio region* interchangeably. When discussing sound edits, they refer to the beginning of a clip as the *header*, the end of the clip as the *tail*, and a specific point within the clip as a *sync point*. The point where two clips are joined is called the *edit seam* (Figure 2.5).

The question of where to cut involves timing and pacing. The question of why to cut involves form and function. When a visual edit interrupts a linear motion such as a walk cycle, the edit jumps out at the audience. *Jump cuts* present a unique challenge for the sound editor in that any attempt to hard sync sound to the linear motion will further advertise the edit. If sound is not required for that specific motion, it is better to leave it out altogether. However, if sound is essential, the sound editor must find a way to *cheat* the

Figure 2.5 Audio Clip Header, Edit Seam, and Tail

sound in an effort to minimize continuity issues. This is a situation where linear music can be used effectively to mask or smooth the visual edit.

TRANSITIONS

Dissolves

A visual *dissolve* is a gradual scene transition using overlap similar to an *audio cross-fade*. Dissolves are used to indicate the passage of time or a change in location. The sonic equivalent of a visual dissolve is an audio cross-fade, a technique commonly used in connection to visual dissolves. In *Antz* (1998), as the male character Z waits excitedly for his love interest Princess Bala to join him on a date, the instrumentation of the underscore gradually thinned through the many dissolves, finally ending on a solo instrument to play his isolation and disappointment for getting stood up.

Wipes

A *wipe* is a transitional device that involves pushing one shot off and pulling the next shot into place. Unlike the dissolve, there is no overlap in a wipe. Blue Sky uses wipes cleverly in the *Ice Age* films, integrating seasonal objects like leaves and snow to re-enforce the passage of time. This approach lends itself to hard effects, BGs, and score. In the *Flintstones* television series, wipes are frequently used and often scored with cues timed specifically to the transition.

Fades

A *fade* uses black to transition the audience in and out of scenes. Fade-outs indicate closure and are timed to allow the audience time to process what has recently transpired. Closure can be supported through music cues that harmonically resolve or cadence. In many episodes of the *Flintstones*, Hoyt Curtain's music cues would half cadence prior to the first commercial break and fully cadence prior to the second commercial break indicating the resolution of the first act. Fade-ins invite the audience into a new scene. BGs, underscore, and dialogue are often introduced off-screen as the film fades in from black. The mixer typically smoothes fade transitions by gradually increasing or decreasing levels in the soundtrack.

Sound Transitions

Not all sound edits are motivated by the literal interpretation of picture edits. As discussed earlier, pre- and post-lap techniques are useful transitional devices. Pre-lapping sound or score to a subsequent scene can be an effective smoothing element when moving between shots, whereas a hard cut of a SFX or BG can advertise the transition and quickly place the audience in a new space. Post-laps allow the audience to continue processing the narrative content or emotion of the preceding scene. In many cases, audio simply *overlaps* from cut to cut. This technique is used for dialogue, SFX, and source music. A *ring-out* on a line of dialogue, music cue, or SFX can be a very subtle way to overlap visual edits. Ring-outs are created by adding reverb at the end of an audio clip, causing the sound to sustain well after the clip has played. This editing technique will be covered more extensively in Chapter 6. Dialogue is sometimes used to *bridge* edits. For example, in *Finding Nemo* (2003), the backstory is delivered through a series of characters handing off the dialogue in mid sentence from cut to cut. With each of these transitional treatments, there are no hard fast rules as to guide the editor. This is why editing is both an art and a craft.

SCENES

Parallel Edit

Parallel editing or *cross cutting* is designed to present two separate but related characters or actions through a series of alternating shots. This editing approach often implies that the actions are occurring simultaneously.

Though the audience is made aware of this relationship, the characters are often unaware; this is an important design consideration. When a music cue plays through the scene, it typically indicates that characters on both sides of the edit are aware of each other and the presenting conflict. If the sound design and score are made to contrast with each cut, this typically indicates that the characters are unaware of their shared experience.

Montage Sequence

A *montage sequence* consists of rapid visual edits designed to compress the narrative. Montage sequences typically feature songs or thematic score with little or no dialogue or SFX. The songs used in montage sequences often contain lyrics that relate to the narrative *(narrative lyrics)*. Songs or thematic score contain melodic lines that create linear motion across the non-linear video edits. In a scene from *Bee Movie* (2007), Barry B Benson falls asleep in the pool of honey. During the dream sequence that follows, Barry's relationship with love interest Vanessa Bloome develops through montage and is scored with the song "Sugar Sugar," a clever play on words.

Time-Lapse and Flashback Sequences

Short form animation often seeks to compress the narrative through the use of temporal devices such as time-lapse and flashback sequences. Time-lapse is an effective means of compressing the narrative. It differs from the montage largely in the way individual shots are transitioned and in its use of diegetic sound. If the sequence does not feature diegetic elements, than underscore is an effective means of promoting continuity. When diegetic elements are the focus of each transition (e.g. a television or radio), then sound edits are often deliberately apparent and designed to exaggerate the passage of time. Flashback sequences are an effective means of delivering backstory. Typically, a flashback sequence has a more subjective look and feel than scenes in the present time. This contrast can be achieved by adding more reverb to the mix or by allowing the underscore to drive the scene (Figure 2.6).

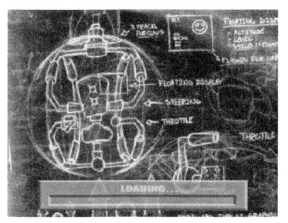
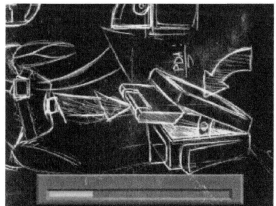

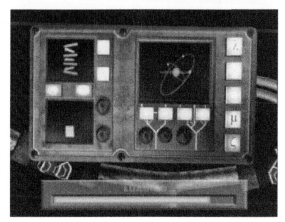

Figure 2.6 This Time Lapse Sequence from Sam (2002) Directed by Kyle Winkleman Shows the Main Character Learning at an Accelerated Speed. Each Cut Was Accompanied by a 35 mm Camera Shutter to Advertise the Edits and EKG Beeps to Represent the Physiologic Impact on the Character

If something works when it "shouldn't" that's when we have to pay attention and try to figure out why. And that's when real learning about editing results.

B.J. Sears

CONCLUSION

The term sound design implies the thought process that begins at the storyboarding stage and continues through the final mix. It is an inclusive approach to soundtrack development that facilitates both technical and creative uses. In film, sound and image are symbiotic. Consequently, sound designers and composers must integrate visual thought into their creative process as animators must integrate aural thought into theirs. The ability to design and execute a film from this mutual perspective will be seen, heard, and, most importantly, felt by the audience.

CHAPTER 3

DIALOGUE

OVERVIEW

Animation has enjoyed a long history of uniquely talented voices infusing personality into their respective characters. One of the earliest known voice artists was Disney himself, serving as the voice of Mickey in *Steamboat Willie* (1928). Artists like Mel Blanc, Daws Butler, and Don Messick devoted their lives to creating the iconic world of talking animals, whereas, Jack Mercer, Mae Questel, and June Foray helped establish the caricature style of voicing humans. As was the case for most voice actors, the characters they voiced would achieve incredible star status yet the public rarely knew the real face behind the voice. Voice actors like Alan Reed (Fred Flintstone) and Nancy Cartwright (Bart Simpson) remain relatively anonymous yet their characters are immediately recognizable throughout the world. The success of features such as *American Tail* (1986) and *The Little Mermaid* (1989) helped usher in a renaissance of animation. During this period, the reputation for animation improved and "A" list actors once again began showing an interest in animation projects. Perhaps the recent success of directors Seth MacFarlane and Brad Bird voicing characters for their films suggests that we are coming full circle. Like Disney, they demonstrate that understanding the character is essential to finding and expressing a persona through voice. To learn more about the voice actors behind animation, log onto www.voicechasers.org.

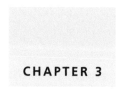

Wait a minute . . .
if I'm not talking,
I'm not in the
movie . . . .

Tom Hanks (*Toy Story*)

PRINCIPAL DIALOGUE

Dialogue is the most direct means of delivering the narrative, and whenever present, becomes the primary focus of the soundtrack. The speaking parts performed by the main characters are referred to as *principal dialogue.* Principal dialogue can be *synchronous* (lip sync) or *a-synchronous* such as off-screen lines or

Figure 3.1 *Elements of the Dialogue Stem*

thoughts shared through voice-over. Some films deliver principal dialogue in a *recitative* (blending of speech and music) style. Two examples of this approach can be heard in the 1954 animation *The Seapreme Court* and the 1993 film *The Nightmare Before Christmas*. With the rare exception of films like *Popeye* (1933), principal dialogue is recorded prior to animating (pre-sync). The dialogue recordings are then used to establish timings, provide a reference for head and body movements, and serve as the foundation for lip sync.

NARRATION

Look, up in the sky, it's a bird; it's a plane, it's Superman.

Jackson Beck

Narration differs from principal dialogue in that the speaker is unseen and cannot be revealed through changes in camera angles. Many animations develop a storybook quality for their projects through the use of narration. Narration is an effective means of introducing the story *(prologue)*, providing back-story, and providing closure *(epilogue)*. The use of narration as an extension of the on-screen character's thoughts is referred to as *first person*. This technique is used effectively in *Hoodwinked!* (2005) to support the Rashomon style of re-telling the plot from multiple perspectives. The *third-person* narration is told from an observer's perspective. Boris Karloff exemplifies this approach in the 1966 version of *How The Grinch Stole Christmas*. When used effectively, audiences will identify with the narrator and feel invited to participate in the story. Even though narration is non-sync, it is still recorded prior to animating and used to establish the timings.

GROUP ADR AND WALLA

If you listen closely to the backgrounds in the restaurant scene in *Monsters, Inc.* (2001), you will hear a variety of off-screen conversations typical of that environment. These non-sync but recognizable language backgrounds are the product of *Group ADR*. Group ADR is performed by a small group of actors (usually 6 to 8) in a studio environment. They are recorded in multiple takes that are combined to effectively enlarge the size of the group. Group actors perform each take with subtle differences to add variation and depth to the scene. Examples of group ADR can be heard as early as 1940 in the Fleisher *Superman* cartoons and later in the 1960s cartoons of Hanna-Barbera. A more recent example can be heard in *Finding Nemo* (2003) during the scene where a flock of sea gulls chant "mine, mine." In this scene, the words are clearly discernable and as such, are included in the dialogue stem. While group ADR is intelligible, Walla is non-descript. Walla is often cut from SFX libraries or recorded in realistic environments with actual crowds. It can effectively establish the size and attitude of a crowd. Due to its non-descript nature, Walla is included in the FX stem.

DEVELOPING THE SCRIPT

The script begins to take shape at the storyboard stage where individual lines are incorporated into specific shots. Once the storyboards are sufficiently developed, an animatic (story reel) and recording script are created. At this early stage, *scratch dialogue* is recorded and cut to the animatic to test each shot. Oftentimes it is fellow animators or amateur voice actors who perform these recordings. In some workflows, professional voice actors are brought in at the onset and allowed to improvise off the basic script. With this approach, it is hoped that each read will be slightly different, providing the director with additional choices in the editing room. Once a shot is approved and the accompanying script is refined, the final dialogue is recorded and edited in preparation for lip sync animation.

CASTING VOICE TALENT

Often when listening to radio programs, we imagine how the radio personalities might appear in person. We develop impressions of their physical traits, age, and ethnicity based entirely on vocal characteristics. When casting voices for animation, we must select voices that will match characters that are yet to be fully realized. We seek vocal performers who can breath life into a character, connect with the audience, and provide models for movement. Voice actors must possess the ability to get into character without the aid of completed animation. Though physical acting is not a primary casting consideration, many productions shoot video of the session to serve as reference for the animation process. It is common practice in feature animation to cast well-known actors from film and television, taking advantage of their established voices. Most independent films lack the resources needed for this approach and must look for more creative means of casting. An initial pool of talent can be identified through local television, radio, and theater. If the budget allows, there are a growing number of online options available for casting and producing voice talent (Figure 3.2).

Though it helped to be physical in front of the microphone . . . in a sense, everything is focused into your voice.

Ray Fines
(*The Prince of Egypt*)

Figure 3.2 *Online Voice Talent Services*

To do is to be.

Socrates

To be is to do.

Jean-Paul Sartre

Do be do be do.

Frank Sinatra

Scoobie Doobie Doo.

Don Messick

CARICATURE

Voice actors are often asked to step outside their natural voices to create a caricature. Mimicry, sweeteners, and regional accents are important tools for developing caricature. *Animal speak* such as the dog-like vocalizations of Scooby Doo or the whale-like speech in *Finding Nemo* are but a few examples of this unique approach to dialogue. In *Stuart Little* (1999), cat hisses are added (sweetened) to Nathan Lane's dialogue to enhance the character of Snowbell, the family cat. In *Aladdin* (1992), Robin Williams' voice morphs from a genie into a sheep while vocalizing the phrase "you baaaaaaaad boy." Regional accents are often used to develop the ethnicity of a character. In *Lady and the Tramp* (1955), the Scottish terrier, the English bulldog, and the Siamese cats are all voiced with accents representative of their namesake. Caricature can add a great deal of depth to a character if used respectfully. It can also create a timbral separation between characters that help make them more readily identifiable in a complex scene.

RECORDING DIALOGUE

THE RECORDING SCRIPT

Animation dialogue begins with a vetted *recording script* (Figure 3.3). Each line of dialogue is broken out by character and given a number that corresponds to the storyboard. The recording script can be sorted by character to facilitate individual recording sessions. Some directors hold rigidly to the recorded script while others show flexibility to varied degrees. Many of the great lines in animation are a result of embellishment or

Figure 3.3
Character Displays his
Flip Book Idea in the
Film The Machine
(2003) Directed by
Jason Davies

Character 1 (Little Orange Guy)

<u>Line 5</u>

(00:03:54:07–00:04:17:12)

I got a plan you see. I'm gonna make a lot more of these machines only bigger. It will make pictures as big as a wall. And they'll tell stories and people will come from all around and give us money to watch them . . . heh!

Character 2 (Large Blue Guy)

<u>Line 7</u>

(00:04:18:03–00:04:19:22)

Your mad.

Character 1

<u>Line 21</u>

(00:04:23:01–00:04:24:17)

What . . . what what whatabout . . .

Character 2

<u>Line 22</u>

(00:04:24:23–00:04:38:04)

That is by far the looniest thing I've ever heard. Look mate, no one will ever want to watch little moving pictures dancing on the walls . . . all right. Much less give some bloody nitwit money for it.

improvisation of a talented voice actor. Since the script is recorded in pre-animation, there still exists the possibility to alter, replace, or add additional lines. Every variation is recorded and re-auditioned in the process of refining and finalizing the dialogue.

DIRECTING VOICE TALENT

Ok, I'd like to do it again . . . ALONE!!!—

Buddy Hackett (*The Little Mermaid*)

Actors that are new to the animation process are often surprised to learn that dialogue is recorded without picture. For many, it is the first time they will rely exclusively on their voice acting to deliver a compelling read. Many arrive at the session prepared to deliver a cartoony voice rather than their natural voice. It is the director's job to help voice actors find the voice best suited for each character. Since their character has not yet been animated, it is important to help the voice actor get inside the character and understand the context for each line. This can be accomplished by providing concept art (Figure 3.4), storyboards, and a brief breakdown of the script. Directors and/or script supervisors often accompany the voice talent in the live room. Their presence should be facilitative and non-threatening. Directors should resist the temptation to micro-manage the session, allowing voice actors flexibility to personalize the script through phrasing, inflection, and non-verbal vocalizations. In some productions, voice actors are encouraged to improvise off-script. The spontaneity and authenticity resulting from this approach can potentially transform a character or a shot. During the session, it is helpful to record in complete passes rather than stopping in mid-phrase to make a correction. By recording through mistakes, we avoid "paralysis through analysis" and the session produces more usable material.

THE ADR STUDIO

It is not uncommon for dialogue to be recorded in Foley stages or in facilities designed for music production. Recording dialogue in a professional facility offers many advantages including well-designed recording spaces, professional grade equipment, and experienced engineering. Because most dialogue is recorded from a close microphone placement (8 to 12 inches), any good sounding room can be transformed into a working studio. The essential components of an ADR studio include a digital audio workstation, quality microphones, audio and video monitors, and basic acoustic treatments. The recording software must support video playback with time code. It is

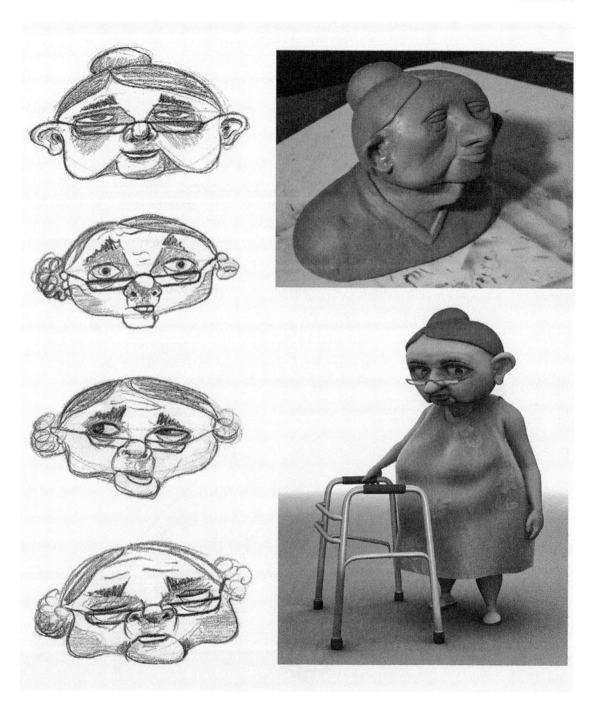

Figure 3.4 *Concept Art from the Film* Trip to Granny's *(2001) Directed by Aaron Conover*

important to select video monitors and computers that are relatively quiet. Whenever possible, they should be isolated from the microphone or positioned at a distance that minimizes leakage. If the room is reverberant, sound blankets can be hung to provide additional dampening and sound isolation.

MICROPHONES

Microphones are the sonic equivalent of a camera, capturing varied degrees of angle (polarity) and focus (frequency and transient response). Most dialogue mixers prefer large diaphragm condenser microphones as they capture the widest frequency range with the greatest dynamic accuracy. The Neumann U-87 microphone is a popular yet pricey choice (Figure 3.5). There are many condenser microphones that meet high professional standards yet are priced to suit smaller budget productions.

The polar pattern of a microphone is analogous to the type of lens used on a camera (Figure 3.6). However, unlike a camera lens, microphones pick up sound from all directions to some degree. The omni-directional pattern picks up sound uniformly from all directions. Consequently, this pattern produces the most natural sound when used in close proximity to the voice talent. Some microphones are designed with switchable patterns allowing for experimentation. Regardless of the pattern selected, it is wise to be

*Figure 3.5 **Neumann U-87 with Pop-filter***

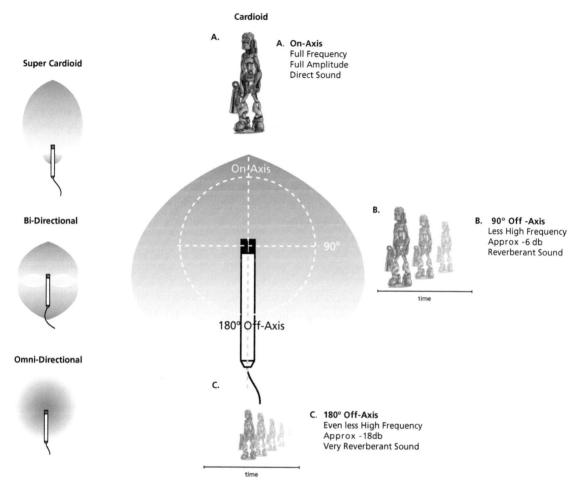

Cardioid

Super Cardioid

Bi-Directional

Omni-Directional

A.

A. **On-Axis**
Full Frequency
Full Amplitude
Direct Sound

On-Axis

90°

180° Off-Axis

B.

B. **90° Off -Axis**
Less High Frequency
Approx -6 db
Reverberant Sound

time

C.

C. **180° Off-Axis**
Even less High Frequency
Approx -18db
Very Reverberant Sound

time

Figure 3.6 The Sound Characteristics Associated with Various Types of Polar Patterns

consistent with that choice from session to session. Whether the dialogue
is intended as scratch or if it will be used in the final soundtrack, avoid using
microphones that are built in to a computer.

RECORDING SET-UP

Principal dialogue is recorded in mono with close microphone placement. The
microphone is pointed at a downward angle with the diaphragm placed just
above the nose. The recording script is placed on a well-lit music stand lined
with sound absorption materials to prevent the unwanted reflections or

rustling sounds. Avoid placing the microphone between the actor and other reflective surface such as computer screens, video monitors, or windows. Improper microphone placement can produce a hollow sounding distortion of the voice known as comb filtering. A *pop-filter* is often inserted between the talent and the microphone to reduce the plosives that occur with words starting with the letters P, B, or T. Headphones are usually required when shooting (recording) ADR with three preparatory beeps; many actors like to keep one ear free so they can hear their voice naturally. In some workflows, multiple characters are recorded simultaneously to capture timings of lines interacting and to allow the actors to react to other performers. With this approach, it is still advisable to mike up each character for greater separation and control in postproduction.

CUEING A SESSION

In pre-animation, scratch takes of principal dialogue are recorded *wild* (non-sync) and cued on a single track by character. Mixers have the option of recording individual takes on nested playlists or multiple audio tracks. With either approach, all takes can be displayed simultaneously. However, the playlist technique conserves track count, makes compositing easier, and provides a convenient track show/hide option. See Chapter 6 for a more detailed explanation on digital cueing and preparatory beeps.

PREPARING TRACKS FOR LIP SYNC

Some directors prefer to keep individual takes intact rather than creating a composite performance. This approach preserves the natural rhythm of each line while also reducing editorial time. In the second approach, multiple takes are play-listed and portions of any given take are rated and promoted to a composite playlist. When compositing dialogue, the most transparent place to cut is during the spaces between words. With this type of edit, the main concerns are matching the level from take-to-take and developing a rhythm that feels natural. If an edit must be made within a word, cutting on the consonants is the most likely edit to preserve transparency. Consonants create short visible waveforms with little or no pitch variations and are easily edited. It is very difficult to match a cut occurring during a vowel sound due to the unpredictable pitch variations that occur from take-to-take. Regardless of the approach used, once the director settles on a take *(circled take),* it is delivered to the animator for track reading.

LIP SYNC ANIMATION

Track reading is an art unto itself. The waveforms displayed in a digital track-reading program represent more sonic events than need be represented visually. Phrases like "Olive Juice" and "I love you" produce similar waveforms unless one places the em fah sis on a different sill ah bull. Animators learn to identify the important stress points and determine what mouth positions are needed to convey the dialogue visually. Track readers map the dialogue on *exposure sheets* like the one shown in Figure 3.7. They scrub the audio files and listen for these stress points, marking specific frames where lip sync needs to hit. At the most basic level, consonants like M, P, and B are represented with a closed mouth position. Vowels are animated with an open mouth position. Traditional animators use exposure sheets or applications like Flipbook to mark specific frames for mouth positions.

In 3D animation, the animator imports the dialogue audio files into the animation software, key framing the timeline at points where lip sync needs to hit. Many animators begin lip sync by animating body gestures and facial expressions that help the audience read the dialogue. They view these gestures and facial expressions as an integral part of the dialogue. When effectively executed, this approach leads the audience to perceive tight sync regardless of the literal placement.

ADR

Once the lip sync animation is completed, any changes to the existing dialogue must be recorded in sync to picture in a process known as ADR or replacement dialogue. When recording replacement dialogue, the editor cues each line to a specific time code location within the character's respective track. Three preparatory beeps are placed in front of the cue at one-second intervals to guide the voice actor's entrance. Alternatively, streamers and punches are overlaid on the video to provide a visual preparation for an entrance. Some DAWs provide a memory location feature useful for cueing ADR digitally (Figure 3.8). With this feature, the location of individual cues can be stored in advance and quickly recalled at the session.

You really can't hone in on the character until you hear the actual voice you're going to have.

James Bresnahan
(Horton Hears a Who!)

Sportscaster

Line 3

(00:00:58:16 - 00:04:17:12)

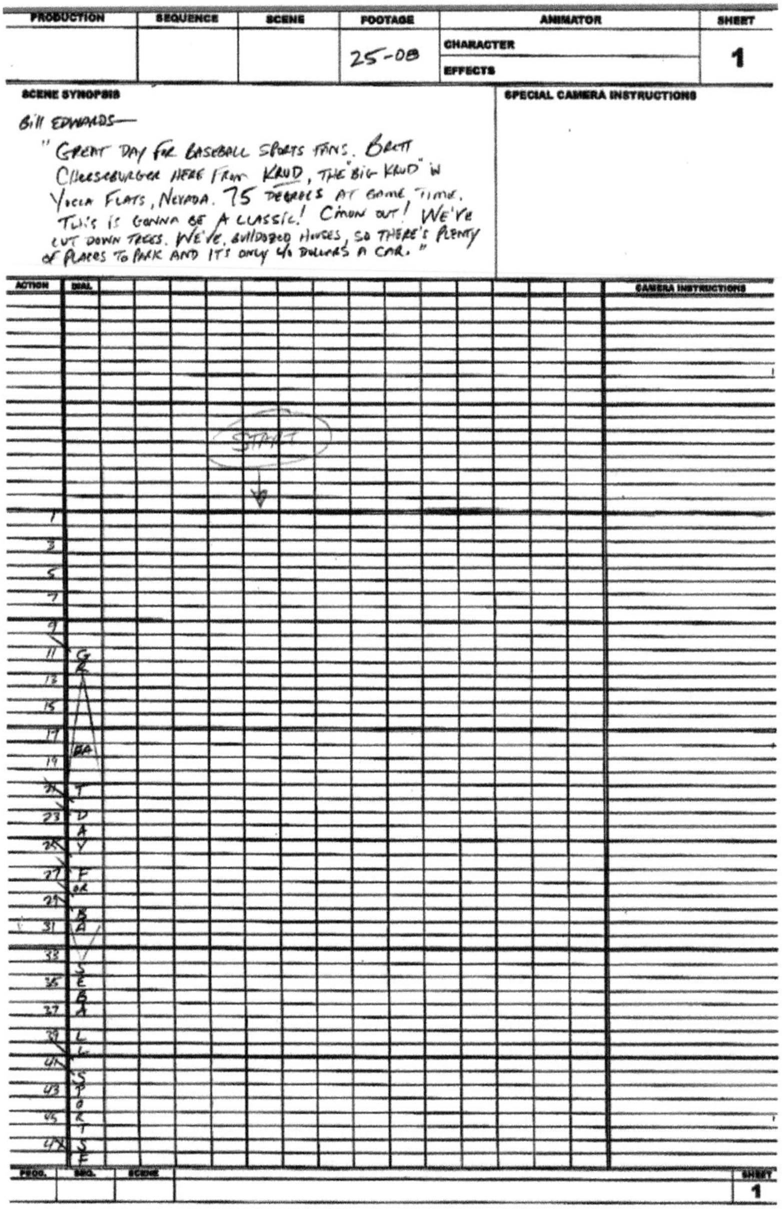
PRODUCTION | SEQUENCE | SCENE | FOOTAGE: 25-08 | ANIMATOR | CHARACTER | EFFECTS | SHEET: 1

SCENE SYNOPSIS

BILL EDWARDS—

"GREAT DAY FOR BASEBALL SPORTS FANS. BRETT CHEESEBURGER HERE FROM KRUD, THE "BIG KRUD" IN YUCCA FLATS, NEVADA. 75 DEGREES AT GAME TIME. THIS IS GONNA BE A CLASSIC! C'MON OUT! WE'VE CUT DOWN TREES. WE'VE BULLDOZED HOUSES, SO THERE'S PLENTY OF PLACES TO PARK AND IT'S ONLY 40 DOLLARS A CAR."

SPECIAL CAMERA INSTRUCTIONS

ACTION | DIAL. | CAMERA INSTRUCTIONS

START

PROD. | SEQ. | SCENE | SHEET 1

Figure 3.7 Exposure Sheet for Pasttime *(2004)*

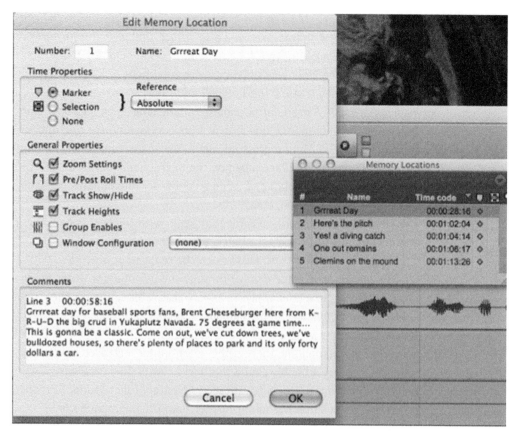

Figure 3.8 Memory Locations for Digital Cues

EVALUATING RECORDED DIALOGUE

Whether recorded as scratch, final dialogue, or ADR, there are many objective criteria for evaluating recorded dialogue. It is the responsibility of the dialogue mixer to ensure that the dialogue is recorded at the highest possible standards. The following is a list of common issues associated with recorded dialogue.

- *Sibilance* – Words that begin with *s, z, ch, ph, sh,* and *th* all produce a hissing sound that, if emphasized, can detract from a reading. Experienced voice talents are quick to move off of these sounds to minimize sibilance. For example, instead of saying "ssssssnake" they would say "snaaaake" maintaining the length while minimizing the offending sibilance. Moving the microphone slightly above or to the side of the talent's mouth (off-axis) will also reduce sibilance. In rare cases, sibilance can be a useful tool for character development. Such was the case with Sterling Holloway's hissing voice treatment of Kaa, the python in the Walt Disney feature *The Jungle Book* (1967).

- *Peak Distortion* – A granular or pixilated sound caused by improper gain staging of the microphone pre-amp or from overloading the microphone with too much SPL (sound pressure level). Adjust the gain staging on the microphone pre-amps, place a pad on the microphone, move the source further from the microphone, if using a condenser microphone, consider a dynamic microphone instead.

- *Plosives (Wind Distortion)* – Words that begin with the letters *b, p, k, d, t,* and *g* produce a rapid release of air pressure that can cause the diaphragm to pop or distort. Plosives can be reduced or prevented with off-axis microphone placement or through the use of a pop-filter. Some takes can be improved by applying a high-pass filter set below the fundamental frequency of the dialogue to reduce plosives.

- *Proximity Effect* – When voice talent is positioned in close proximity to a directional microphone, there is the potential for increased bass response, causing a boomy sound that lacks clarity. This *proximity effect* is sometimes used to advantage to create a fuller sound. To reduce this effect, re-position the talent further from the microphone or consider using an omni-directional pattern. A bass roll-off or high-pass filter (Figure 3.9) can also be used to effectively manage proximity effect.

- *Nerve-related Problems* – Recording in a studio is intimidating for many actors. The sense of permanence and a desire for perfection often produce levels of anxiety that can impact performance. Signs of anxiety include exaggerated breathing, dry mouth, and hurried reading. It is often helpful to show the talent how editing can be used to composite a performance. Once they learn that the final performance can be derived from the best elements of individual takes, they typically relax and take the risks needed to deliver a compelling performance.

- *Lip and Tongue Clacks* – Air conditioning and nerves can cause the actor's mouth to dry out. This in turn causes the lip and tongue tissue to stick to the inside of the mouth, creating an audible sound when they separate. Always provide water for the talent throughout the session and

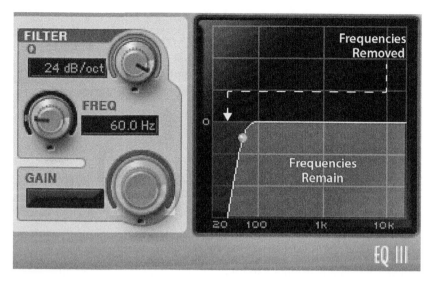

Figure 3.9 Bass Roll-Off

encourage voice actors to refrain from drinking dairy products prior to the session.

- *Extraneous Sounds* — Sounds from computer fans, florescent lights, HVAC, and home appliances can often bleed into the recordings and should be addressed prior to each session. In addition, audible cloth and jewelry sounds may be captured by the microphone due to close placement of the microphone to the talent. It is equally important to listen for unwanted sound when recording dialogue.

- *Phase Issues* — Phase issues arise when the voice reflects off a surface such as a script, music stand, or window and is re-introduced into the microphone. The time difference (phase) of the two signals combine to produce a hollow or synthetic sound. Phase can be controlled by repositioning the microphone and placing sound absorbing material on the music stand.

- *Extreme Variations in Dynamic Range* — Variations in volume within a vocal performance contribute greatly to the expressive quality and interpretation. Unfortunately, dialogue performed at lower levels often gets lost in the mix. Equally problematic is dialogue performed at such high levels as to distort the signal at the microphone or pre-amp. A compressor is used to correct issues involving dynamic range. Compressors will be covered at greater length in Chapter 7.

- *Handling Noise* — Handling noise results when the talent is allowed to hold the microphone. Subtle finger movements against the microphone casing translate to thuddy percussive sounds. The actors should not handle microphones during a dialogue session. Instead, the microphone should be hung in a shock-mounted microphone cradle attached to a quality microphone stand.

DIALOGUE EDITING

You want to create the illusion of tight sync without losing the feel.

David Stone

The dialogue editor is responsible for cleaning tracks, compositing takes, tightening sync, and preparing tracks for delivery to the mix stage. Even when recorded in studio conditions, dialogue tracks often contain environmental noise, rustling of paper, cloth sounds, headphone bleed, and extraneous comments from the voice actor. The dialogue editor removes these unwanted sounds using a variety of editing and signal processing techniques. Dialogue editors are also responsible for tightening the sync for ADR and foreign dubs. Even the most experienced voice actors have difficulty matching the exact rhythm of the original dialogue. Dialogue editors resolve sync issues using editing techniques and time compression/expansion (TC/E) software. Most DAWs come with TC/E plug-ins to facilitate manual sync adjustments. However, specialized plug-ins such as Vocalign were developed specifically for tightening lip sync. Vocalign maps the transients of the original dialogue and applies discrete time compression/expansion to the replacement dialogue. For foreign dubs, Vocalign has a sync point feature that allows the user to align specific words from both takes (Figure 3.10). Once the editing and signal processing is completed, the dialogue editor consolidates and organizes the tracks in a manner that is most facilitative for the mixing process.

DESIGNED LANGUAGES

Some animations call for a designed or *simulated language*, such as the alien language of the Drej in *Titan A.E.* (2000). Simulated dialogue establishes plausible communication in the context of a fantasy. One common approach is to reverse an existing line of dialogue (Figure 3.11). The resultant line contains a logical structure but lacks intelligibility.

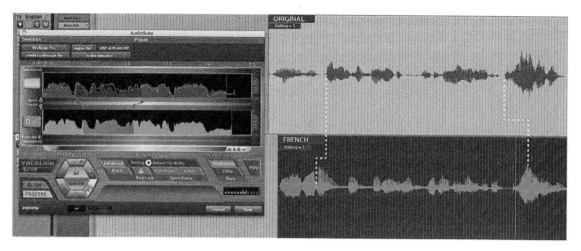

Figure 3.10 Vocalign Is Applied to a Foreign Dub Using the Sync Point Feature to Aligned Specific Words

Original

Figure 3.11
Reversed Dialogue

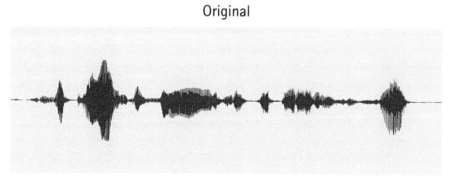

"So what kind of ahh ya know audition is this heh?"

Reversed

"Heys ahs in ahh shid no oh dee of vewd nyadh govuse"

Since the resultant dialogue is unintelligible, subtitles are often added to provide a translation. Signal processing is yet another design tool used to transform dialogue for effect. The familiar robotic sounds heard in films like *Wall-E* (2008) are achieved by processing ordinary dialogue with Vocorders, harmonizers, and other morphing plug-ins.

Some approaches, though less technical in execution, are equally effective. For example, the adult voices in Charlie Brown's world are mimicked with brass instruments performed with plungers. With this approach, communication is implied while minimizing the presence of adults. The humorous *Flatulla* dialect heard in *Treasure Planet* (2002) was achieved by combining armpit farts with a variety of vocal effects. In the 1935 Silly Symphony *Music Land,* lifelike musical instruments inhabit the Land of Symphony and the Isle of Jazz. Rather than mime the narrative, director Wilfred Jackson chose to represent dialogue with musical phrases performed in a speech-like manner. *Music Land* is an entertaining attempt at making us believe that music is truly a universal language, capable of bridging any Sea of Discord.

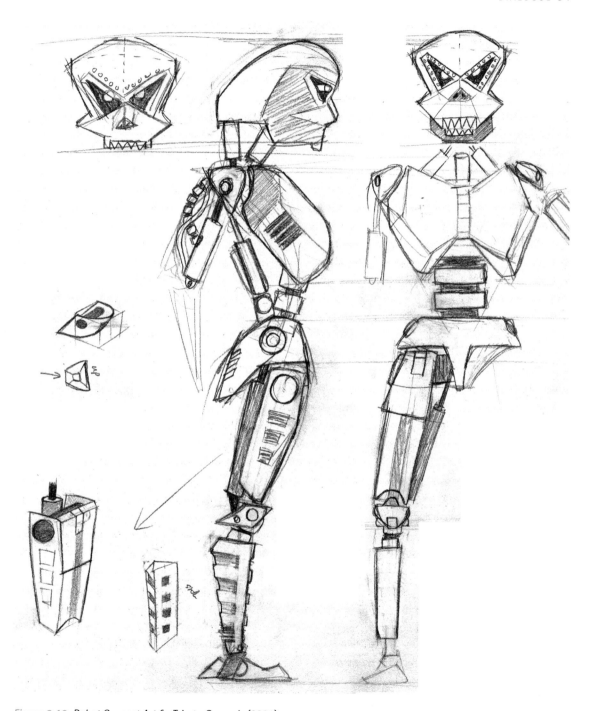

Figure 3.12 Robot Concept Art for Trip to Granny's (2001)

CHAPTER 4

MUSIC

OVERVIEW

The music stem or *score* is perhaps the most difficult component of the soundtrack to describe in words. Ironically, score rather than SFX often drive films that lack dialogue. Each musical entrance in a soundtrack is called a *cue*. A cue can *underscore* a scene or represent a *source* such as a radio or phonograph. In addition to source and underscore, many films use music for title,

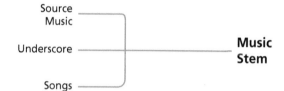

Figure 4.1 Elements in the Music Stem

montage, and end credit sequences. The labeling convention for a cue is 1M1, the first number representing the reel and the last number representing the order in which it occurs. Cues are often given titles representative of the scenes they accompany. The blueprint for the score is created at the *spotting session* that occurs immediately after *picture lock* (no further picture editing). Film *composers* begin scoring immediately after the spotting session and are expected to compose two to five minutes of music each day. If copy-protected music is being considered, a *music supervisor* is brought in at the earliest stage to pursue legal clearance. The *music editor* has responsibilities for developing cue sheets, creating temp tracks, editing, synchronization, and preparing the score for the re-recording mixer. There are many additional roles related to the development of the score such as orchestrators, musicians, music contractors, and recording engineers.

> People sing when they are too emotional to talk anymore.
>
> Lynn Ahrens (*Anastasia*)

UNDERSCORE

During the golden age of animation, underscore was anything but subtle. Most of the action on and off-screen was covered by musical cues that were often indistinguishable from the SFX stem. Composers of this era pioneered

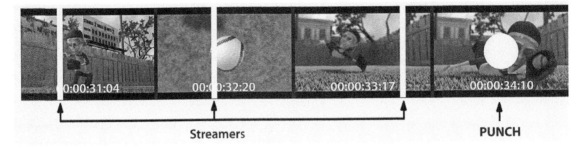

Figure 4.2 White Vertical Lines Stream across the Frames toward the Circular Punch where the Score Will Hit with the Action

> I'm a storyteller . . . and more or less in the food chain of the filmmaking process, I'm the last guy that gets a crack at helping the story.
>
> James Horner

the integration of twentieth-century musical styles and performance techniques. Even though they pushed the musical boundaries, their scores remained both playful and accessible. In contemporary animation, the style and approach of underscore is oftentimes indistinguishable from live action cues. Underscore can play through a scene or hit with specific action. Cues that play through a scene provide a linear element in the soundtrack, smoothing edits and creating emotional continuity within a scene. The practice of hitting the action with musical accents is a long established convention. In addition to hitting the action, musical cues occasionally hit with dialogue as well. For example, in the film *Anastasia* (1997), Comrade Phlegmenkoff's line "And be grateful, too" is punctuated with orchestral chords to add emotional weight to the delivery.

SOURCE MUSIC

Source music is the diegetic use of songs to contribute to the implied reality of the scene. To maintain this realistic feel, source music is often introduced "in progress," as if the audience were randomly tuning in. Songs are commonly used as source material, effectively establishing time period, developing characters, or acting as a cultural signifier. Source music also supports time-lapse sequences by changing literally with each shot. Source music can be either on-screen (emitting from a radio or phonograph) or off-screen (such as elevator music or a public address system). The songs used in source music are almost always selected for their lyric connection to the narrative. Source music is processed or *futzed* to match the sonic characteristics of implied sound source. Like hard effects, source music is treated like a SFX and panned literally to the on-screen position. Cues often morph or transition from *source to underscore* to reflect the narrative shift in reality typified by montage sequences and other subjective moments.

SONGS

During the golden age of animation, familiar songs were routinely quoted instrumentally, and the implied lyrics were integral to the sight gags. Original songs such as "Some Day My Prince Will Come" from *Snow White* (1934) blended narrative lyrics with score to create a *musical monologue*. Walt Disney Studios was largely responsible for the animated musical, developing fairy tale stories around a series of songs performed by the characters. These songs are *pre-scored*, providing essential timings for character movements and lip sync. In animated musicals, it is not uncommon for a character's speaking voice to be covered by a voice actor while the singing voice is performed by a trained vocalist. Great care is taken to match the speaking voice with the singing voice. An effective example of this casting approach can be heard in *Anastasia*, where Meg Ryan's speaking voice flawlessly transitions to Liz Callaway's vocals. A more recent trend in animation is the use of pre-existing songs as the basis for the score. This is known as a *song score*; examples of this approach include *Shrek* (2001), *Lilo and Stitch* (2002), and *Chicken Little* (2005). It is sometimes desirable to create a new arrangement of an existing tune as a means of updating the style or customizing the lyrics. An example of this occurs in *Jimmy Neutron: Boy Genius* (2001) in a montage sequence where Thomas Dolby's "She Blinded Me with Science" is covered by Melissa Lefton singing "He Blinded Me with Science" to reflect the POV of Cindy Vortex (Jimmy's female adversary/love interest). Songs continue to play an important roll in short form independent animation, especially if the film does not incorporate dialogue. However, there are potential risks associated with the use of songs in animation. Songs can give a film a dated feel over time, which is why the accompaniments of songs in animated musicals are primarily orchestral. They also introduce the potential for copyright infringement, an issue that will be addressed later in this chapter.

TITLE, MONTAGE, AND END CREDIT SEQUENCES

Title, montage, and end credit sequences have a unique function in film and present unique scoring opportunities. Title sequence music can effectively establish the scale, genre, and emotional tone of the film. Composers can

> Story is the most important thing . . . not the song as a song, but the song as development.
>
> Richard Sherman

> You gotta have a montage!—
>
> Gary Johnston (*Team America*)

write in a more thematic style, as there is little or no dialogue to work around. A good example of title sequence music can be heard in *101 Dalmatians* (1961). Here the music moves isomorphically and frequently hits in a manner that foreshadows the playful chaos that will soon follow. Montage sequences are almost always scored with songs containing narrative lyrics. The linear nature of songs and their narrative lyric help promote continuity across the numerous visual edits comprising a montage sequence. End credit music should maintain the tone and style established in earlier cues while also promoting closure. The end-credit score for animated musicals often consists of musical reprises re-arranged in modern pop styles suitable for radio play.

WORKFLOW FOR ORIGINAL SCORE

RATIONALE FOR ORIGINAL SCORE

> I aim in each score to write a score that has its own personality.
>
> Alan Menken

Directors often seek an original score that is exclusive, tailored, and free from preexisting associations. Original music can be an important tool for branding a film. The iconic themes and underscore heard in the Hanna-Barbera animations cannot be emulated without the drawing comparison. Original cues are tailored with hits and emotional shifts that are conceived directly for the picture. In concert music, there are many standard forms that composers use to organize their compositions. If these conventions were used as the basis for film scoring, form and tempo would be imposed on the film rather than evolving in response to the images. Music is known to encapsulate our thoughts and feelings associated with previous experiences. Filmmakers seek to avoid these associations and create unique experiences for their audience. With original score, cues can be written in a similar style without evoking past associations. Even when the music is of a specific style or period, it can be scored to create a timeless feel.

TEMP MUSIC

Temp music is perhaps the most effective vehicle for communicating the type of score required for a specific film. As the name implies, a temp (temporary) track is not intended for inclusion in the final soundtrack. Temp tracks are edited from pre-existing music to guide the picture editing process, facilitate test screenings, and provide a musical reference for the composer. The responsibility of creating a temp track often falls on a picture or sound editor. Editors select music that matches the style and dramatic needs as represented in the storyboards or animatic. The music is then edited and synced to create a customized feel for the score. Because the temp track is for internal use, copy-protected material is often utilized. Temp tracks can prove problematic if the director becomes overly attached and has difficulty accepting the original score.

THE SPOTTING SESSION

In animation, cues can be source, pre-score, or non-sync underscore. Pre-scored cues must be developed before the animation process begins as the characters are moving in sync to the musical beats. Some composers prefer to begin writing thematic material and underscore for the film as early as the storyboarding stage. However, most underscore cues are decided once the picture is locked. Here, the director meets with the composer and music editor to screen the film and discuss where music can best be contributing. The spotting session is an important opportunity for the director to clarify their vision for their film on a shot-by-shot basis. If a temp score exists, these cues are played for the composer to help clarify the style and intent. During the spotting session, the music editor takes detailed notes related to specific cues (Figure 4.3). From these notes, the music editor generates cue sheets outlining the parameters of each cue.

> Before you can set out and start scoring . . . one's gotta be on the same page with the filmmakers.
>
> Harry Gregson-Williams (*Flushed Away*)

Suggestions for identifying cues in a spotting session:

- Determine the importance of music for the scene.
- Look for opportunities in the scene where music can be brought in without drawing attention to itself.
- Decide when the music should hit, comment, or play through the action.

Music Spotting Log

Date. _____

Page No. _____

Project Title: _____   Composer: _____

Music Editor: _____

Cue #:	Cue Name:	Notes:
Start Time: : : :		
End Time: : : :		
Total Time: : : :		

Figure 4.3 Spotting Log Template

- Be selective; wall-to-wall music tends to lose its effectiveness.
- Be open to all musical styles; allow the image, rather than personal taste, to influence decisions.

WRITING ORIGINAL CUES

> My job is to make every moment of the film and every frame of the film come to life.
>
> John Debney

Film composers must be able to write in all styles and for a wide range of instruments. Chord progressions, rhythmic patterns, and instrumentation are elements that can be emulated to capture the essence of the temp track. They are often used to provide the foundation for an original theme resulting in a similar, yet legal cue. Today, most films are scored to digital video using extensive sample libraries that emulate a wide range of instrumentation. Much of the writing occurs in a project studio utilizing MIDI technologies, recording, and editing capabilities to fully produce each cue. The composer does not work directly with the animator when writing individual cues. Instead, they meet periodically to audition and approve individual cues. Composers use the feedback gained from these sessions to hone in on the musical direction for individual cues. It is important to note that additional picture edits occurring after this point can result in significant qualitative, budget, and scheduling implications. Most scores are created as *works for hire*, requiring the composer to surrender publishing rights to the production company. Creative fees are negotiated based on experience and the amount of music required. Smaller budget projects often require the composer to handle all tasks associated with producing the score. This type of contract is referred to as a *package deal*, and includes: orchestration, part writing, contracting musicians, recording, conducting, and music editing.

THE SCORING SESSION

Sample libraries have steadily improved, providing composers with access to a comprehensive set of orchestral, rock, and ethnic samples from which to orchestrate their cues. However, sample-based scoring can be time consuming and lack the expression and feel created with live musicians. Consequently, many larger projects use the traditional approach using live musicians at a *scoring session*. The space where the cues are recorded is called a *scoring stage*. Scoring sessions involve many people and resources, so planning is an important means of optimizing resources. The music editor attends the scoring session(s) to run the clock (synchronization) and to help evaluate individual takes. Due to budget realities and the limited access to qualified musicians, the blending of sequenced music with live musicians is becoming a common practice for a wide range of projects. Once the cues are completed, they are delivered to the music editor for additional editing and sync adjustments. From there, the tracks are delivered to the re-recording mixer in preparation for the final mix

WORKFLOW FOR PRODUCTION LIBRARIES

PRODUCTION LIBRARIES

Hoyt Curtain (composer for Hanna-Barbera) developed a distinctive in-house music library for shows such as *The Flintstones* and *The Jetsons*. The cues contained in this library were re-used in subsequent seasons as well as other series. This provided Hanna-Barbera with a low cost music approach to scoring that also contributed to the continuity while promoting their brand. Commercially available *production libraries* have been developed for similar purpose. The days of "canned music" have long since passed and modern production libraries are providing a high quality, low cost, and expedient means of developing specialized cues or an entire score. The music tracks

Figure 4.4 Production Music Library from DeWolfe, available on disks or hard drive.

contained in commercial libraries are *pre-cleared* for use on audio/visual productions. Low-resolution audio files can be downloaded and cut into the temp, allowing the client to approve the cues in context. There are some disadvantages to production music including non-exclusivity, the need for costly editing, and the lack of variation for specific cues. The three types of production libraries are classified by their licensing specifications. *Buy-out* libraries are purchased for a one-time fee and grant the owner unrestricted use. *Blanket licensing* covers a specified use of a library for an entire project. *Needle drops* are the third and most expensive type of library. Needle drop fees are assigned per cue based on variables such as length, territory, distribution, and nature of the use. Most blanket and needle drop libraries provide online search, preview, delivery, and payment options.

SEARCHING A LIBRARY

As with all scores, the process begins with a spotting session to determine where cues are needed and the nature of individual cues. This information guides the music editor in searching production libraries for musical selections that might potentially become music cues. Commercial production libraries can be rather expansive, containing thousands of hours of music. Most production companies have online search engines to assist the music editor in a search. Categories, keywords, and musical styles are the most common type of search modes (Figure 4.5). Categories are broad and include headings such as Instrumentation, Film Styles, National/Ethnic, and Sports. Keyword searches match words found in titles and individual cue descriptions. Emotional terms prove to be most effective when searching with keywords. Musical styles are also common to production library search engines. Many musical styles are straightforward but others are more difficult to distinguish. This is particularly true of contemporary styles such as rock, pop, and hip-hop. If you are unfamiliar with a particular style, find someone who is and get them to validate the style.

Figure 4.5 APM and DeWolfe Search Categories

MANAGING A PROJECT

Many online libraries contain a project management component in their browsers (Figure 4.6). This feature allows the music editor to *pull* individual cuts from the library and organize them by specific projects and cues. As with original score, there comes a point in the project where the director is brought in to approve the cues. The music editor can open a specific project and play potential cuts directly from the browser. Alternatively, they can download tracks and cut them to picture, allowing the director to audition and approve each cue in context (Figure 4.7).

Figure 4.6 Three Potential Cuts Saved in APM's Project Manager

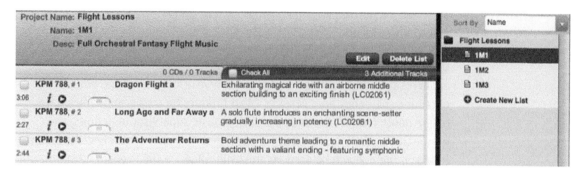

Figure 4.7 Playlists Containing Three Potential Music Cues for "Flight Lessons" Directed by Neil Helm (2010). These Cues Were Downloaded in Full Resolution from the APM Library

DEVELOPING CUES

A skilled music editor can edit cues to create the illusion that the music was scored for a particular scene. They do this by matching the emotional quality of a scene, conforming cues to picture, and developing sync points. Oftentimes, it is the editing that "sells" a particular music selection. Once the cues are developed, the director is brought in to audition and approve the cue. Many of the techniques used by the music editors are also used by dialogue and SFX editors and will be discussed in greater length in Chapter 8.

LICENSING CUES

Once the final placement of the music is determined and the director approves the cue, the music editor or supervisor completes the process by obtaining the necessary licensing. Most production music companies have online quote request forms to assist the music supervisor in defining the nature of the use (Figure 4.8). It is important to accurately define the extent to which the cue will be used, as this will influence the licensing fee. Licensing parameters can always be expanded at a later time at an additional cost. Once licensing fees are determined, an invoice is issued to the music editor or production company. This invoice constitutes the formal agreement that becomes binding when payment is received.

WORKFLOW FOR COPY-PROTECTED MUSIC

OVERVIEW

A verbal contract isn't worth the paper it's written on.

Samuel Goldwyn

Where animation is subjective, arts law is objective, requiring the artist to fully comply with the international laws pertaining to copyright. The digital age has provided consumers with unprecedented access to digital media. The ease and extent to which this content can be acquired has led to a false sense of entitlement by consumers. It is easy for student and independent filmmakers to feel insulated from issues associated with copyright infringement; however, the potential consequences are substantial regardless of the size or nature of the project. It is the role of the *music supervisor* to clear copy-protected music for use in a film. In Dreamworks' *Shrek* films, the music supervisor cleared an average of 14 copy-protected cues per film. This

PROJECT INFORMATION

Client Name:
Production Title: *
Production Length: *
Episode #:
Network:
P.O. #/Job #:
License Application: *   Feb ⬥ 08 ⬥ 2012 ⬥
Estimated Airdate/Release Date:

BROADCAST PROGRAMS:

	Per Needledrop	Blanket 30 min.	60 min.
All Media excluding Theatrical	☐	☐	☐
All TV and For Sale Media	☐	☐	☐
All TV Media	☐	☐	☐
Free TV (U.S. & Canada only)	☐	☐	☐
Cable/DBS TV	☐	☐	☐
Radio/Satellite Radio	☐	☐	☐
Internet Program (Webisode)	☐	☐	☐
Personal Use/Mobile Device	☐	☐	☐
In-Transit Exhibition	☐	☐	☐

THEATRICAL/THEME PARK/MUSEUM:

	Per Needledrop
Broad Theatrical Rights, over $10 million	☐
Broad Theatrical Rights, less than $10 million	☐
Broad Theatrical Rights, less than $5 million	☐
Theatrical Exhibition only	☐
Film Festival only	☐
Trailer: Broad Rights, Theatrical Campaign	☐
Trailer: Broadcast Campaign	☐
Trailer: Broad Rights, Single Trailer	☐
Trailer: For Sale Media, Single Trailer	☐
Stadium or Theme Park	☐
Museum	☐

PROMOS:

Show:
First Line of Copy:

☐ One version only   Length of Version:
☐ Multiple Versions   For Multiple versions, indicate quantity per version

_____ :60   _____ :30   _____ :15   _____ :10   Other (specify)

	Worldwide	National / Unlimited	National / 13-week	Regional	Local
All Media, ex. Theatrical	☐				
All TV Media	☐	☐	☐	☐	☐
Free TV		☐	☐	☐	☐
Cable/DBS TV		☐	☐	☐	☐
Radio	☐	☐	☐	☐	☐
In-Theater	☐				
Internet	☐				
Personal Use/Mobile Media Device	☐	☐	☐	☐	☐

INTERNET USAGE:

	Per Needledrop	Blanket 15 min.	30 min.	60 min.
Internet Program (Webisode)	☐	☐	☐	☐
Embedded Web page Use	☐			

Figure 4.8 *Online Request Form for APM*

section is designed to provide guidelines for music clearance. As with any legal endeavor, if in doubt, obtain the services of an arts lawyer.

RIGHTS VERSUS LICENSE

When seeking to license copy-protected music, it is important to clarify what specific permissions you are requesting from the copyright holder. For scoring purposes, copyright law only applies to melodies and lyrics. Chord progressions, accompaniment figures, and instrumentation are not protected and can be freely used without risk of copyright infringement. Copyright holders have the exclusive right to reproduce, publish, license, or sell their melodies and lyrics. They also have the right to grant permission, set licensing

Every great film composer knows where to steal from.

Richard Stone
(*Animaniacs*)

fees, and establish terms for any music synced to picture. A publisher often controls the synchronization rights and the record companies typically hold the master rights.

SYNCHRONIZATION, MASTER, AND VIDEOGRAM LICENSE

There are three specific licenses of primary concern to the music supervisor; the *synchronization license*, the *master license*, and the *videogram license*. The synchronization license is the most important of the three, for if this license is not granted, the music cannot be used on the film in any form. The synchronization license grants the right to sync copy-protected music to moving picture. A synchronization license is granted at the discretion of the copyright owner, who is typically the composer or publisher. To use a specific recording of a song requires a master license, which is often controlled by a record company. To make copies of the film for any form of distribution requires videogram licensing. The videogram license must be obtained by both the publisher and record company if a copy-protected recording is used. Licensing can be time consuming and there are no guarantees. Therefore, it is prudent to begin this process as early as possible.

PUBLIC DOMAIN

Works that are public domain can be used freely in an animation. Any music written before January 1, 1923 is public domain. Works written after that date can enter public domain if the term of the copyright expires. Use of the copyright notice (©) became optional on March 1, 1989. It is up to the music supervisor to ensure that a given selection is in fact public domain. One way to establish public domain is to search the selection at www.copyright.gov. Once material is in the public domain, exclusive rights to the work cannot be secured. It is important to differentiate public domain from *master rights*. Although the music contained on a recording might be public domain, the master rights for the actual recording is usually copy protected.

FAIR USE

The authors of the Copyright Act recognized that exceptions involving non-secured permission were necessary to promote the very creativity that the Act was designed to protect. The Copyright Act set forth guidelines governing the use of copy-protected material without securing permission from the copyright holder. These guidelines for nonexclusive rights constitute *fair use*:

> The fair use of a copyrighted work . . . for purposes such as criticism, comment, teaching . . . scholarship, or research, is not an infringement of copyright.

In determining whether a specific use applies, consider the following:

- Is the nature of the use commercial value or educational (demonstrating an acquired skill). Even in educational settings, the use of copy-protected music for the entertainment value does not constitute fair use, even if there are no related financial transactions.
- The amount and importance of the portion used in relation to the copyrighted work as a whole.
- The effect of the use on the potential market for, or value of, the copyrighted work. Even if you are not selling the work, distribution, exposure, and unwanted association with a project can have significant impact on the market value of a musical composition.

If an animation complies with these principles, there is strong support for claiming fair use. When claiming fair use, it is still advisable to limit the distribution and exhibition of the work, credit the authors, and display the author's copyright notice within your work. It is important to keep in mind that fair use is not a law but rather a form of legal defense. With that in mind, it is wise to use it sparingly.

PARODY

Parody is an art form that can only exist by using work that is already familiar to the target audience; therefore, provisions had to be made in the Copyright Act for parody or this form of expression would cease to exist. Parody involves the imitation of a recognizable copy-protected work to create a commentary on that work. The commentary does not have to serve academic purposes; it can be for entertainment value. However, both the presentation and the content must be altered or it is not considered a parody. For example, just changing a few words while retaining the same basic meaning does not constitute parody. Parody must be done in a context that does not devalue the original copy-protected work; therefore, parody is most justifiable when the target audience is vastly different than the original. A parody constitutes a new and copyrightable work based on a previously copyrighted work. Because parody involves criticism, copyright owners rarely grant permission to parody. If you ask permission and are denied, you run the additional risk of litigation if you use it anyway. In the United States, fair use can be used successfully to defend parody as long as the primary motive for the parody is artistic expression rather than commercialism. A good example of parody can be heard in the *Family Guy* "Wasted Talent" episode (2000) featuring "Pure Inebriation," a parody on "Pure Imagination" from *Willie Wonka & the Chocolate Factory* (1971).

MUSIC SUPERVISION

When requesting any type of licensing, it is important to define the parameters of your request. Because you will likely pay for licensing based on the scope of the request, it is wise to limit the scope to only that which is needed. The following are basic guidelines when requesting a quote for licensing.

- *Identify the copyright holder.* The publisher usually holds synchronization rights. In most cases, the administrator for this license can be identified through a BMI, ASCAP, or SESAC title search (Figure 4.9). The master rights are often held by the record company.
- *Define the territory* (e.g., local, regional, national, worldwide, national television, national cable, Internet, film festival). This parameter can be expanded if the film becomes more successful.
- *Define the term.* If you are a student, then your participation in student films typically is limited to 12 months after your graduation date. If you want to have the rights to use the piece forever, you should request "perpetuity for the term." Remember, the greater the request, the more you can expect to pay and the greater the chance your request will be denied.
- *Define the nature of use* (e.g., broadcast, student festival, distribution, or sale). This information should include the amount of the material to be

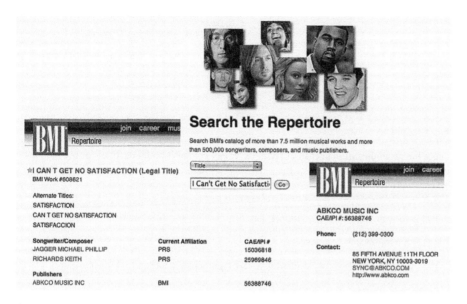

Figure 4.9 A Search for the Rolling Stones Title "I Can't Get No Satisfaction" Using the BMI Search Engine

used (expressed in exact time), where it will be placed in the animation, and the purpose for using it (e.g., narrative lyric quality, emotional amplification, or establishing a time period or location).

- *When stating the budget for the project, clarify whether the published figure is for the production as a whole or for the music only.* The distribution of money varies greatly from project to project. Typically, less than 10 percent of the total film budget is available for scoring.

- *Consider these requests as formal documents read by lawyers and other trained arts management personnel.* Use formal language, and proof the final draft for potential errors. Phrase all communication in such a way that places you in the best position to negotiate. Keep in mind that the law demands precision.

HISTORICAL TRENDS IN ANIMATION SCORING

THE GOLDEN AGE

In 1928, Walt Disney released his first sound animation, *Steamboat Willie*, an animated short driven primarily by score. Within a decade, Carl Stalling and Scott Bradley established a unique style of cartoon music through their

Licensing Quote Request

Month/Day/Year

To: Director of Licensing (use formal name and title)

From: Name and Title (e.g., Music Supervisor)

Re: Project Title by [Director's Name]

I would like to obtain a quote for synchronization license of [Writer's Name] composition [Song Title] for use on the above-titled animation. The details and parameters of the request are as follows:

Nature of use:

1. Specify whether the project is for commercial or educational use.

2. Specify the length of the cue in minutes and seconds.

3. Specify where the animation will be exhibited (e.g., student festivals, commercial advertising, broadcast, or Internet).

4. Specify all details relating to distribution.

5. Specify whether the request is for exclusive or nonexclusive rights.

Production information:

The soundtrack budget is typically less than 10% of the entire budget. Some license administrators will ask you to state the budget for the project.

Term:

The period of time for which the license applies, such as 1 year (as in the case of student films) or for the life of the copyright (as in the case of a commercial release).

Territory:

Clearly define where the animation will be exhibited such as locally, regionally, nationally, or internationally.

Synopsis:

Provide a *brief* summary of the story and discuss how the song contributes to the story.

Contact information:

Phone

Fax

E-mail

Figure 4.10 This Form Contains Most of the Information Fields Required when Making a Licensing Request for Synchronization, Master, and Videogram Licensing

respective work with Warner Brothers and MGM. This music featured harsh dissonance, rapid changes in tempo, exaggerated performance techniques, and quotations from popular tunes. Stalling and Bradley both had a propensity for hitting the action with music, an approach that would become known as *Mickey Mousing*. Though Raymond Scott never scored an animation, his music, especially "Powerhouse," had a profound influence on this musical style and can be heard in many of Carl Stallings scores. Many of the early animations featured *wall-to-wall* (nonstop) music that functioned as both underscore and SFX. Not all animation of the Golden Age featured this approach to scoring. The early Fleisher animations were dialogue driven and contained fewer sight gags. These animations were scored using a more thematic approach associated with live-action films. Winston Sharples and Sammy Timberg composed or supervised many of these scores for films like *Popeye* and *Superman*.

THE TELEVISION AGE

The arrival of television in the late 1940s signaled the end of the Golden Age of animation. As animation migrated to television, decreased budgets and compressed timelines gave rise to a new approach to scoring. Hanna-Barbera emerged as the primary animation studio for this emerging medium. They employed Hoyt Curtain to create the musical style for their episodic animations. As a jingle writer, Curtain had a talent for writing melodic themes with a strong hook. He applied this talent to create some of the most memorable title themes, including *The Flintstones*, *Johnny Quest*, and *The Jetsons*. He also created in-house *music libraries* used consistently from episode to episode. These libraries accelerated production time, cut costs, and gave the studio a signature sound.

THE ANIMATION RENAISSANCE

In 1989, Disney released *The Little Mermaid*, which featured an original song score by composer Alan Menkin and lyricist Tim Rice. In that same year, Alan Silvestri composed the score for *Who Framed Roger Rabbit?* Both films were financially successful and renewed studio interest in feature-length animation. In 1995, Pixar released their first feature animation *Toy Story*, scored by Randy Newman. By the mid-1990s, Alf Clausen had established *parody scoring* as a familiar element of *The Simpsons*. Clausen's skill at parody is well represented in the episode entitled "Two Dozen and One Greyhounds," which features the song "See My Vest," a parody of Disney's "Be Our Guest." Feature animation continues to emphasize scoring, attracting A-list composers, editors, and supervisors.

CHAPTER 5

SOUND EFFECTS (SFX)

OVERVIEW

Animation provides the sound editorial department with a silent backdrop from which to create a sonic world. Whether cutting hard effects, developing backgrounds, creating design elements, or recording Foley effects, the absence of production audio associated with live action film is often liberating. As with score, readily identifiable styles of FX and Foley have emerged that are associated with innovated sound designers, production companies, and animation genres. The use of sound effects for dramatic purposes can be traced back to ancient Greek theater. In the beginning of the twentieth century, Radio Theater became the primary outlet for storytelling. The techniques developed for Radio Theater would become the foundation for sound in cinema. Treg Brown and Jimmy MacDonald are two of the earliest known sound designers. Brown is known for his creative blending of subjective and realistic sounds to create the unique SFX style associated with the early Warner Brothers animation. Jimmy MacDonald is remembered for developing many of the innovated sound making devices that can be heard in decades of Disney classics. In the 1950s, Wes Harrison "Mr. Sound Effects" demonstrated the power of *vocalizations* that can be heard in many of the Disney and MGM productions of that decade. Wes proved that many of the best SFX are found

> Thanks to the movies, gunfire has always sounded unreal to me, even when being fired at.
>
> Peter Ustinov

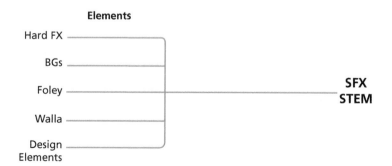

Figure 5.1
Elements Contributing to the SFX Stem

right under our noses. When Hanna and Barbera left MGM, they brought a large portion of the SFX library used for *Tom and Jerry* with them. With the help of Pat Foley and Greg Watson, Hanna and Barbera developed one of the most iconic SFX libraries in the history of animation. Contemporary sound designers such as Gary Rydstrom, Randy Thom, Ben Burtt, and Dane Davis continue the strong tradition established by these innovators.

THE SFX STEM

> The challenging thing about the animated film is that you have to entirely invent the world.
>
> Randy Thom

The SFX stem is divided into several layers including *hard effects, Foley, backgrounds (BGs), Walla,* and *Design Elements.* Together, these layers are responsible for the majority of the tracks comprising a soundtrack. Hard effects and Foley cover much of the basic sounds and movements in the soundtrack. Hard effects differ from Foley in that they are cut or edited rather than performed. Foley is such an important element in animation that it will be discussed in a separate chapter. Until recently, backgrounds (BGs) were rarely used in animation and underscore often provided the environmental background. Today, BGs are a common element in the soundtrack, providing the sonic backdrop for the animated world. In the opening sequence of Disney's *Dinosaur* (2000), notice the many different BGs represented as the Iguanodon egg travels through the multitude of environments. In Pixar's *Toy Story,* the backgrounds heard outside Andy's window support his warm and playful nature. In contrast, the backgrounds accompanying Sid accentuate his sadistic and edgy qualities. Walla, though built on non-descript dialogue, functions in a similar fashion to backgrounds and is included in the SFX stem. As the name implies, design elements are created by layering sounds to cover sonically complex objects critical to the narrative.

TEMP TRACKS AND SPOTTING SESSIONS

Animation differs from live action in that sound editorial need not wait for picture lock to begin soundtrack development. Temp FX, scratch dialogue, and temp music are useful when developing shots and scenes with an animatic. They help establish timings, mood, and environments, while providing important story points that may not be visually represented. Temp effects provide additional feedback for motion tests such as walk cycles and accelerating objects. As the animation process nears completion, the film is screened *(spotting session)* with the director, the supervising sound editor, and lead sound editors to finalize SFX and dialogue for the film. Since the soundtrack for an animation is entirely constructed, every sound is deliberate. Important considerations for the inclusion of sound are:

- Is the sound object important to the narrative or is it ambient?
- Is the sound object intended to support realism or fantasy?
- What are the physical characteristics of the sound object?
- How does the sound object move or interact in the environment?
- Are there any existing models to base the design on?

THE SOUND DEPARTMENT

The sound department is responsible for the development of SFX and Dialogue Stems. The head of the sound editorial department is the *supervising sound editor.* The Sups ("soups") are responsible for assembling a crew, developing and managing the audio budget, developing a post-production schedule, developing a workflow, making creative decisions, and insuring that the delivery requirements are properly met. Additional *FX, Dialogue, and Foley editors* are brought in based on post-production demands, schedules, and available budget. For larger projects, the supervising sound editor may appoint individual editors to take a lead or supervising role in each area. *Sound designers* are enlisted to create the creative design elements. *Foley* and *dialogue mixers* are enlisted to record *Foley walkers* and *voice actors.*

> You learn that the most important thing that you can do as a sound designer is to make the right choice for the right sound at the right moment in a film.
>
> Ben Burtt

SOUND EDITORS

Sound editors cut or edit *elements (SFX)* and *dialogue* to picture. They are responsible for insuring that audio properly syncs to image and conforms in length. Sound editors are also responsible for cleaning up the tracks and re-conforming the soundtrack when additional picture edits are made. There are two basic workflows for sound editing. The first involves assigning individual reels to editors who are responsible for all of the elements within that reel. In the second workflow, editors are given responsibility for specific elements across multiple reels. The first approach is useful when schedules are compressed; the second approach facilitates continuity from reel-to-reel. The lead or Supervising SFX, Dialog, and Foley editors are also asked to cue sessions for ADR and Foley as well as preparing the tracks for the mix stage.

> If I find a sound isn't working within a scene, I'll abandon the science and go with what works emotionally.
>
> Ben Burtt

COMMERCIAL SFX LIBRARIES

Many of the sounds that editors cut to picture are pulled from commercial SFX libraries (Figure 5.2). These libraries are expedient and cost effective, containing hard-to-obtain sounds such as military equipment, dangerous animals, and historical props. As such, they are a practical reality in modern media production. Database software has been developed for the specific purpose of managing these extensive libraries. They contain search engines that recognize the unique metadata associated with sound effects. In addition, they allow the sound editor to preview individual sounds and transfer them to media editing software. Numerous delivery formats are in use for commercial sound effects, including *CDs*, *preloaded hard drives*, and *on-line delivery*. Hollywood Edge, Sound Ideas, and SoundStorm are three popular SFX libraries that deliver in CD and hard drive formats. Individual SFX can also be purchased online at www.sounddogs.com and www.audiolicense.net.

Figure 5.2 Commercial SFX Libraries Are a Practical Reality in Media Production

All of the major commercial libraries are licensed as *buyouts*, meaning the SFX can be used on any media project at no additional cost. There are many sites on the Internet offering free SFX downloads: many of these sites contain highly compressed files taken from copy-protected libraries. Therefore to get the best quality and to protect the project from infringement, additional care should be taken when using files obtained in this manner.

SEARCHING SFX LIBRARIES

In the early years, individual sound effects were stored on film and cataloged using note cards. Today, we can store thousands of hours of SFX on a single drive and access them using customized database software. To effectively search a SFX library, the sound editor must acquire a very specialized vocabulary and some basic search techniques (Figure 5.4).

Most search engines use Boolean logic which utilizes three basic qualifiers to narrow a search; and, or, and not. To narrow a search and to make the search results dependent on the presence of multiple keywords, use AND in conjunction with keywords (e.g., GLASS AND BREAKING). To expand a search utilizing independent keywords, use OR in conjunction with keywords (e.g., GLASS OR BREAKING). To narrow a search and exclude specific keywords, use NOT in conjunction with keywords (e.g., NOT BREAKING). Parentheses allow users to combine AND, OR, and NOT in the search; for example, GLASS AND (PLATE NOT EYE) will produce a more refined result. Placing quotations on a group of terms focuses the search to specific phrases that contain all

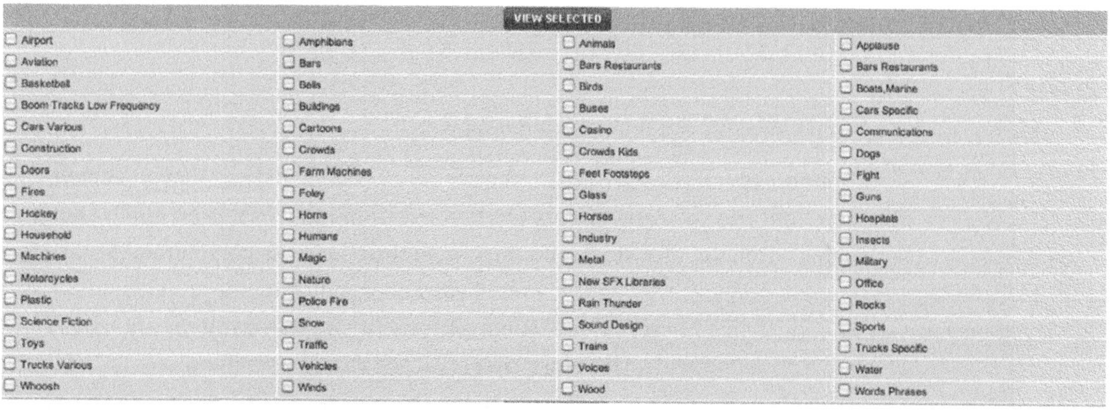

Figure 5.3 Categories in the SoundDogs Online Library

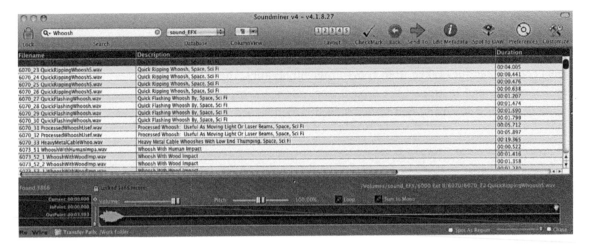

Figure 5.4 *The Search Engine for Soundminer*

keywords in sequence; for example, GLASS AND BREAKING can yield a
multitude of off-target results, but "GLASS BREAKING" greatly limits the search.
You can combine keyword searching with phrase searching as well (e.g.,
LAUGHTER AND "LARGE AUDIENCE"). The Soundminer application has a unique
feature called *lock search* that allows the user to refine the search with
subsequent keywords (Figure 5.5). For example when searching guns in the
database shown in Figure 5.5, we get 3,534 search results. By locking down
the search and typing the Glock modifier, we refine the search to 91 results.
The modifiers 9 mm and Single Shot refine the search to 49 and 28 returns,
respectively.

DEVELOPING AN ORIGINAL SFX LIBRARY

CREATING AN ORIGINAL LIBRARY

Commercial libraries are cost effective and convenient, but they also have
their limitations. Many effects are derived from low-resolution audio sources
such as archival film stock and aged magnetic tape. As commercial libraries,
they are non-exclusive and can be heard on a multitude of projects. In
addition, some library effects (such as those of Hanna-Barbera) are icons for
well-known projects, therefore users run the risk of attaching unwanted
associations to new projects. For these reasons, many SFX editors prefer to
record original sound effects uniquely suited to a specific project. Sound

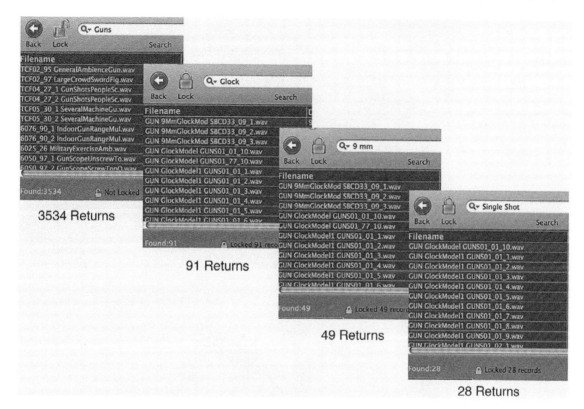

Figure 5.5 *Narrowing Results using a Locked Search*

effects can be recorded in a studio under controlled conditions or in the field. A sound editor armed with a digital recorder, microphones, and headphones can capture a limitless number of recordings. Many great sound effects are obtained by accident, but not without effort.

FIELD RECORDERS

Hard disc recorders provide a practical solution to a variety of recording needs including field acquisition of SFX (Figure 5.6). These recorders can capture audio at high bit-depths and sampling rates in file formats supported by most audio editing software applications. The field recorders shown in Figure 5.6 are battery operated for increased mobility. They utilize a file based storage system which facilitates immediate transfer using the drag and drop method. The Zoom features built-in microphones, alleviating the need for additional microphone cables.

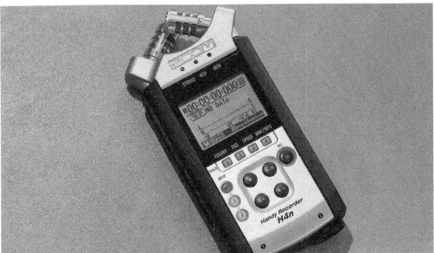

Figure 5.6 The H4n Zoom and Sound Device Hard Disc Recorders Used in Field SFX Acquisition

FIELD MICROPHONES

Microphone selection and placement represent the first of many creative decisions required to effectively capture SFX. The choice between a dynamic and condenser microphone comes down to transient response, frequency response, sensitivity, and dynamic range. The *dynamic microphone* is most effective for close positioning of a microphone on a loud signal. *Condenser microphones* are most effective at capturing sounds containing wide frequency and dynamic ranges and are particularly useful in capturing sources from greater distances. The polar pattern on a microphone is analogous to the lens type on a camera. Cardioid patterns are more directional and reject sounds from the side and the back, and are therefore useful when sound isolation is needed. Omni-directional microphones pick up sound evenly at 360 degrees, capturing a more natural sound but with additional environmental noise. Some microphones have built-in high-pass filters to minimize wind noise, low-frequency rumble, and proximity effect. Many sounds can only be obtained from a distance, requiring highly directional microphones like the shotgun and parabolic microphones.

FIELD ACCESSORIES

When field recording, it is wise to remember that you only have what you bring with you in your kit, so plan carefully. The following is a list of accessories that are useful for the many situations that can arise in the field.

a. Microphone cables come in a variety of lengths. It is a good practice to include cables of varied lengths in your field kit. A three-foot cable is useful for hand-held microphones, while longer cables are needed for boom pole work and multiple microphone placements from varied distances.

b. Field recording without *headphones* is like taking a photograph with your eyes closed. Headphones reveal sound issues such as handling noise, wind noise, and microphone overloading that are not indicated on the input meters. Headphones also bring to the foreground sounds to which our ears have become desensitized, such as breathing, cloth movements, and footsteps. Headphones should sufficiently cover the ears and have a good frequency response. The earbuds used for portable music devices are not sufficient for this purpose. The windscreens that come with most microphones provide limited protection from the low frequency noise caused by wind.

c. The *wind sock* is effective at reducing wind distortion with minimum impact on frequency response (Figure 5.7). Wind socks are essential for outdoor recording, even when conditions are relatively calm.

d. There are many uses for a *boom pole* outside of its traditional role in live-action production audio (Figure 5.8). Boom poles are thin and lightweight and can be varied in length to overcome physical barriers that effect

Figure 5.7 *Wind Sock on Short Shotgun Microphone*

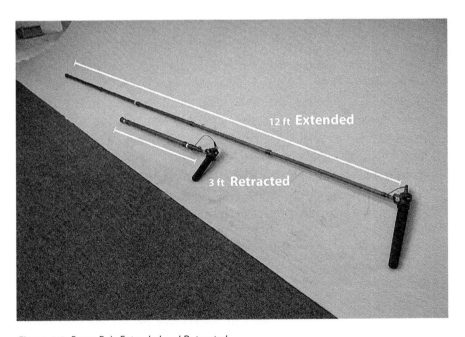

Figure 5.8 *Boom Pole Extended and Retracted*

Figure 5.9 Shock Mount and Pistol Grip

microphone placement. They can also be used to sweep a sound object, effectively recording movements without changing perspective.

e. S*hock mounts* and padded *pistol grips* are used to isolate the microphone handling noise (Figure 5.9). Shock mounts can be attached to pistol grips or boom poles.

f. Moisture has an adverse effect on the performance and life of microphones and recording equipment. Humidity and condensation can be a particular problem, causing static pops in the signal. *Zip Lock Bags, sealable plastic containers,* and *Silicone Gel Packs* take up very little space, help organize equipment, and provide protection against moisture related issues. Often when you are recording in natural environments, biting insects can become a distraction. If you use bug spray, avoid brands that use DEET as this chemical is very corrosive when it comes in contact with electronic equipment. Always bring an extra supply of batteries.

SUGGESTIONS FOR FIELD RECORDING

Record like an Editor

The purpose of field recording is to create a library that is useful for sound editing. Record with that in mind, leaving sufficient handles after each take, recording with multiple perspectives, and varied performances.

Objectivity

Often when we go into the field to record, we listen so intently for the sound that we are trying to capture that we fail to notice other sounds that if recorded, may render the take unusable. Our ability to filter out certain sounds while focusing on others is known as the *cocktail effect.* It is important for the field recordists to remain objective at all times and to record additional safety takes to guard against this perceptual phenomenon.

Area-Specific Frequency Response

The placement of the microphone too close to an object produces an *area-specific frequency response* that makes the resulting sound hard to identify. Consider the context and proximity by which most audiences experience a specific object and use that information to base your initial microphone placement. Most sound objects are bright and articulate on-axis and progressively darker and rounder as you move off-axis (Figure 5.10).

Signal-To-Noise Ratio

The world is filled with extraneous sounds that make it increasingly challenging to capture clean recordings. The balance between the wanted sound (signal) and the unwanted sound (noise) is referred to as *signal-to-noise ratio* (*S/N ratio*). Selecting remote locations or recording during quiet hours can minimize these issues.

Dynamic Range

Field effects recordists should be familiar with the *dynamic range* (volume limitations) of their equipment and the volume potential of the signals being recorded. *Distortion* results when the presenting signal overloads the capacity of either the microphone or recorder. In digital audio, distortion is not a gradual

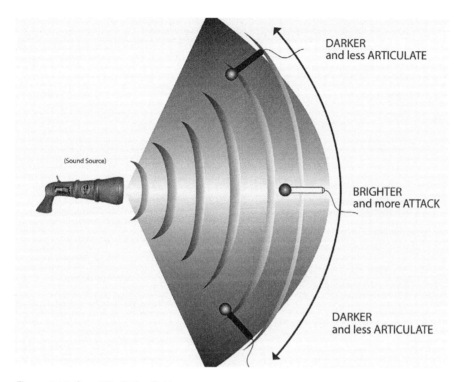

DARKER
and less ARTICULATE

(Sound Source)

BRIGHTER
and more ATTACK

DARKER
and less ARTICULATE

Figure 5.10 Sound Radiation Pattern

process; therefore, when setting microphone levels, it is important to create additional headroom in anticipation for the occasional jumps in volume that often occur. A good starting point is -12 dBfs. For sounds that are not easily repeated, consider using a multiple-microphone approach that takes advantage of varied microphone types, polar patterns, placements, and trim levels.

FILE MANAGEMENT

Field recording is time intensive, often yielding only a relatively small percentage of the usable material. As sound transfers and cataloging do not always occur immediately after a shoot, it can sometimes be difficult to recall the specifics of individual takes. For this reason, many field recordists place a *vocal slate* at the beginning or end (tail slate) of each take. A vocal slate can include any information (metadata) that will become affixed to the file in a database. Figure 5.11 shows many of the metadata fields associated with SFX management software.

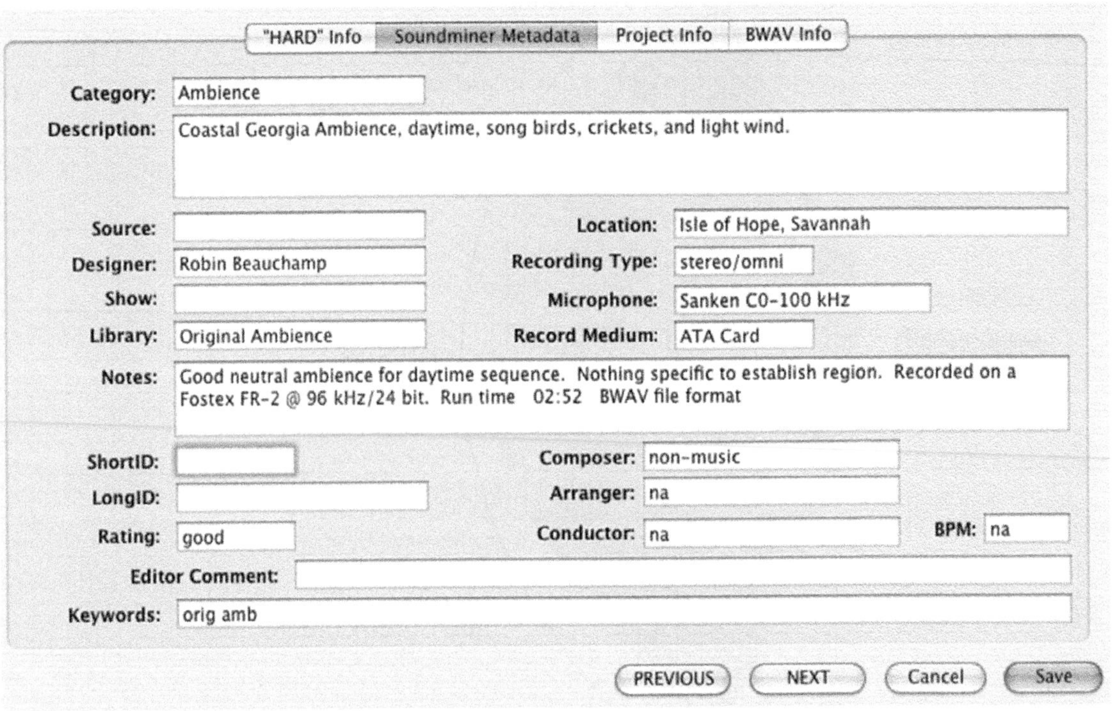

Figure 5.11 Soundminer Metadata

THE SOUND DESIGNER

Sound objects that are complex or subjective in nature often require more creative approaches to their design. The job of creating *design elements* is assigned to highly experienced sound editors, known as *sound designers*. Sound designers use techniques that transcend editing and include sampling, MIDI, synthesis, and signal processing. Examples of design elements include fictitious weaponry, futuristic vehicles, or characters that are either imagined or have ceased to exist. Design elements are typically built-up or layered from a variety of individual elements. It is important to develop an understanding of how characters or objects interact in the environment, what they are made of, and their role in the narrative. When creating a design element, it is also important to deconstruct the sound object to identify all related sounds associated with the object or event; for example, a customized gun sound might be derived from any or all of the key elements shown in Table 5.1

> The trick is to make the sounds useful to the scene, but not make them so attention getting that they snap you out of the movie.
>
> Randy Thom

Table 5.1 Individual Elements of a Cinematic Gun

Ricochet	Bullet trail	Trigger	Projectile
Bullet drop	Cocking	Firing pin	Handling noise
Bullet buzz	Loading	Recoil	Safety release
Bullet zip			

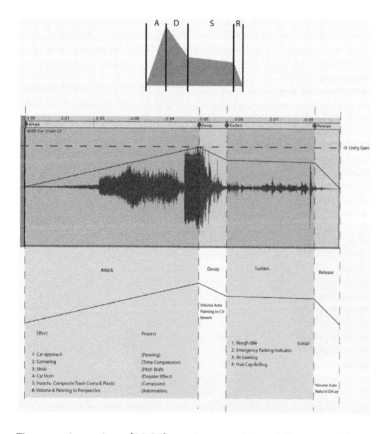

Figure 5.12
ADSR

The sound envelope (ADSR) can be a useful tool for organizing the individual layers that comprise a design element (Figure 5.12). Once each element is identified, sounds can be pulled from a library and combined through editing.

PERFORMING DESIGN ELEMENTS

Since the 1980s, sound designers have been using sampling technology such as the Synclavier to create and perform complex design elements. This approach can be emulated today using software (virtual) samplers and a MIDI

I'm often creating "chords" of sounds.

Wade Wilson
(*Shark Tale*)

keyboard (Figure 5.14). Once the individual elements for the object are identified and pulled from a library, they are assigned to specific keys on a MIDI controller. Multiple samples can be assigned to a single key and triggered discretely based with varied key velocities. Sounds mapped to a specific key will play back at the original pitch and speed. However, they can also be assigned to multiple keys to facilitate pitch and speed variations. Various components of the design element can be strategically grouped on the keyboard, allowing the sound designer to layer a variety of sounds simultaneously. For this approach, systematic file labeling is required to insure the proper key and velocity mapping. For example C#3_Glassshards_03 indicates that the glass shard will be assigned to C#3 on the keyboard and be triggered at the 3rd highest velocity setting. Once a patch is created, individual elements can be performed to image, creating with a multitude of variations in an efficient and organic manner.

Figure 5.13 The Magnetic Giant from the Film Cueb *(2010) Shooting Fragments of Its Body at the Space Traveler. The Sounds Used to Represent the Creature's Movements Were Performed using a Sampler Triggered by a Keyboard*

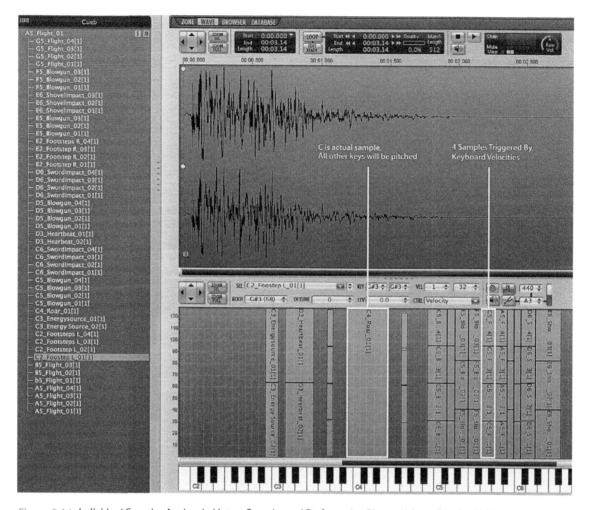

Figure 5.14 *Individual Samples Are Loaded into a Sampler and Performed to Picture Using a Standard MIDI Keyboard*

CHAPTER 6

FOLEY

OVERVIEW

Foley is to SFX what ADR is to dialogue, bringing synchronized performance to the movements of individual characters. This technique is named after Jack Foley who created and applied this approach on many of the films he worked on for Universal Studios. There are three basic types of Foley: *Footsteps*, *Prop Handling*, and *Cloth Movement*. Each of these elements is performed by *Foley artists* who possess a keen sense of timing and a creative approach to selecting and manipulating props. Foley is recorded on a *Foley stage*, outfitted with a variety of walking surfaces called *Foley pits*. The recording engineer for the Foley session is called the *Foley mixer*. In increasingly rare sessions, an assistant engineer called a *Foley recordist* is hired to handle logistics. The *Foley editor* is responsible for cleaning up the Foley cues, tightening up the sync, and organizing the session for pre-dubbing.

THE FOLEY STAGE

Those familiar with the polished look of commercial recording facilities might be taken back by the appearance of a Foley stage (Figure 6.1). The towering collection of props gives the appearance of an un-kept garage rather than a high-end production facility. A functioning Foley stage can be constructed with modest means. Many Foley stages are designed with a live room for the Foley artist and a control room for the Foley mixer. Both rooms are treated acoustically to minimize reverberation. To minimize unwanted noise, computers, projectors, and other competing sounds are placed in an isolated machine room. Vaulted ceilings accommodate projection/video screens and oversized props. Foley pits can be built on top of existing flooring or sunken into the flooring (Figure 6.2). Prop storage with adequate shelving is in

Figure 6.1 Foley Stage at Sound One, New York. Photo Courtesy: Sound One/CSS Studios, LLC

constant demand. At the heart of the control room is the DAW (digital audio workstation), the audio interface, and a basic mixing console. As Foley is recorded on relatively few tracks at any given time, there is no need for the large consoles associated with film mixing or scoring sessions. A limited number of high quality microphones and pre-amps are sufficient and can serve equally well for Voiceover and ADR. The audio software used in Foley must support video playback and basic cueing functions. A small pair of speakers can provide an adequate level of talkback to facilitate the session. Always place your best speakers in the control room so the mixer can hear potential issues with individual takes.

Figure 6.2 Foley Pits

SPOTTING FOLEY

As with music cues, Foley is recorded in post-production. When spotting a film for SFX, the question often arises as to whether to record Foley or cut the effect. The decision to Foley often comes down to the need for a performance in sync to picture. Foley is the logical choice for effects that are either too complex or too specific to be cut from a library. The performance element of this technique yields organic timings and interactions that are impractical with most editing techniques and production schedules. In some cases, cut effects and Foley effects are combined or "married." For example, the sound of a gun firing is a cut effect while the handling of the gun, shells dropping to the ground, and flesh impacts are Foley effects. A supervising Foley editor can readily identify which cues require Foley and cue the session appropriately.

> If it's asteroids exploding and rocket ships flying by, that wouldn't be us. We carry the reels that have a lot of people that are moving, and walking, and doing stuff.
>
> Dennie Thorpe

THE FOLEY ARTIST

Foley artists are physical actors who possess a strong sense of timing and a keen understanding of dramatic nuance. Dancers and musicians tend to excel in this field as they can break a scene down into rhythmic subdivisions and match their performance to these complex patterns. Foley artists often perform in pairs, especially if layered sounds or character interaction is required. They develop a unique vocabulary to describe the sounds they create (onomatopoeia), for example, "I need a more gushy splat here." Foley artists are responsible for selecting the props used. They work with the Foley mixer to determine which takes are most suited for individual cues.

FOOTSTEPS

> Once we get in our shoe, we're kinda in that character.
>
> Zane D. Bruce
> (Men in Black)

Footsteps, human or otherwise, are Foley effects, performed by the artist's feet or hands. In traditional animation, footsteps were often covered by music cues or sound making devices creating the classic sneak step. In contemporary animation, footsteps are being represented with greater realism. For example, the sound of a tiny mouse nervously scurrying across the kitchen floor is performed by the Foley artist patting individual footsteps with their hands. Then, as the giant man enters the room, the Foley artist straps on an oversized pair of boots and stomps about on a representative Foley pit. When a Foley artist walks a character, we are often able to determine the size, age, gender, and emotional state of that character without ever seeing the image. This dimension of character development is at the core of why we record Foley.

PROPS

Foley artists are as creative at selecting props as they are performing them. They spend countless hours auditioning shoes, props, and cloth to develop their personalized repertoire. When they select the "perfect" prop to support a character's movement, there is a sonic gestalt created which makes the prop inseparable from the action. Props are to the Foley artist what a SFX

Figure 6.3 Foley Footsteps from the Film Cueb *(2010) Directed by Alex Knoll*

library is to the sound editor. Their collection grows over time and represents the individual aesthetic and technique of the Foley artists. An attempt to list every prop used in cinema would be futile and many of the best props are kept secret by the Foley artists. Table 6.1 shows an abbreviated list of props essential to any Foley prop room.

Table 6.1 Props for a Foley Prop Room

Shoes/Boots of all types and sizes (Footsteps)
Coffee Grounds and Sand (Grit for Foley Pits)
Latex Gloves (Stretch Sounds)
Wood Dowel's of varied length and diameter (whoosh sticks)
Fishing Pole Tips (Whooshes)
Jump ropes (Whooshes)
Umbrellas (Open/Close Effects, whooshes, wing flaps)
Cloth of various types (Whooshes, Cloth Pass)
Leather Jacket (Body Impacts)
Book Bags and Canvas Travel Bags (Body Impacts)
Velcro and Zippers (Open/Close)
Dishwashing Soap (Mucus or Sticky Sounds)
Chamois Cloth and Toilet Paper (Wet Effects like Splats)
Wintergreen Life Savers (Bones Cracking)
Knives and Sharpeners (Cutting and Sword Play)
Rubber Bands (Cartoon Footsteps)
Balloons (Stretch, Rub, Squeal, and Pop Effects)
Boxes of nails (Shaking Effects)
Popcorn, beans, and rice (Pouring Effects)
Paint and Make Up Brushes (Brush Effects/Wing Flaps)
Rolls of Tape (Extending Sounds) Measuring Tape (Retracting Sounds)
Hinges (Mechanical/ Squeak Effects)
Wicker Baskets/Chairs (Creaking Sounds)
Spray Paint Can w/nozzles removed (Shakes or Cartoon Footsteps)
Compressed Air and Bicycle Pump (Open/Close Effects)
Pill Bottles (Open/Close)
Bending Straws (Bending, Bubbling Effects)
Wine Bottles (Cork Pops)
Wind up Clocks, Fishing Reels, and Ratchet Wrenches (Mechanical Rotation)
Cigarette Lighter (Lighting Fuses or Cigarettes)
Coins, washers, Car Keys (Personal Effects)
Pens that clip, Pencils (Writing, On/Off Switches)
Paper of different weights (Tearing and Writing)
Computer Keyboards and Manual Typewriters (Keyboard Foley, Miniature Footsteps)
2 × 4's (Wood Cracks, Bat Cracks)
Firearm Shell Casings of varied caliber (Gun Foley)
¼ Inch Magnetic Tape, VCR Tape, 35 mm Film (Rustling Sounds)
Cinder Blocks/Bricks (Large Objects Moving)

When creating a production budget, don't forget to include Foley prop acquisition in the equation.

THE CLOTH PASS

The cloth pass is the last Foley element to be recorded and is typically done in a single take or pass. The practice of performing a cloth pass in animation is relatively new. The primary purpose of the cloth pass is to provide a subtle life-like feeling for individual characters. While props are specific, the cloth pass is more generic, and Foley artists focus on the larger eye catching movements. By recording the cloth pass on a separate track, the mixer can play the cloth at very low levels. The cloth track is typically panned in the center channel of the mix to blend with the dialogue. Featured cloth movements such as a leather jacket or a villain's cape are recorded on a separate track and mixed in the same fashion as props.

CUEING A SESSION

> The best Foley Artists learn to be discriminating . . . to help focus the scene with the Foley, not clutter it.
>
> Vanessa Theme Ament (*The Foley Grail*)

Once the Foley cues are decided at the spotting stage, the supervising Foley editor begins to cue the session. In digital workflows, individual cues are built into the session (Figure 6.4).

In this approach, the cueing process begins with an edit selection that encompasses the length of the cue. The edit selection is then consolidated to create a separate region that is visible on the track. Once consolidated, the region is labeled to reflect the specific prop used. The cue is then stored in a memory location that also includes general viewing properties and a comments window (Figures 6.5 and 6.6). The information stored in the comments window can be extracted to create a traditional cue sheet.

THE FOLEY MIXER

OVERVIEW

The Foley mixer must have proficiency with recording technologies, a good eye and ear for sync, and good communication skills. As mixers, their first task is to import the pre-cued session, adjust the I/O, and assign microphones to the track inputs. There are varied opinions regarding microphone selection and placement. Since animation does not have to match production effects

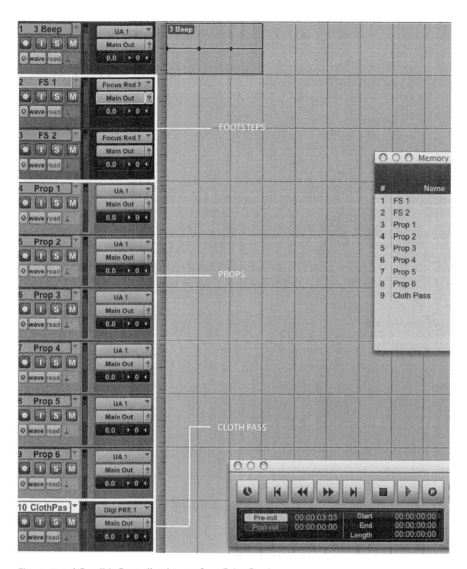

Figure 6.4 A Possible Recording Layout for a Foley Session

(PFX), there is less need for using production microphones or to record with perspective. The MKH 416 (more common to production audio) and the Neumann U87 are favored for both Foley and ADR. There is no codified workflow dictating how a Foley session should run. Instead, the mixer works with the Foley artists to develop recording procedures that suit the working style of both. Some artists prefer to walk the footsteps of an entire character

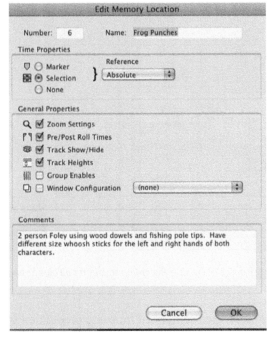

Figures 6.5 and 6.6
A Cue and Its Associated Memory
Location. Notice that the Comment
Section Has Information that Might
Be Found in a Traditional Cue Sheet

moving from surface to surface. This approach helps the artist stay in character and achieve a flow. This approach is also helpful to the editor and mixer by having all of the footsteps for an individual character located on a single track. Some Foley artists prefer to use separate takes or tracks when using multiple surfaces. This first approach is useful when the surfaces are not conveniently positioned or when different footwear is required.

RECORDING WITH PREPARATORY CUES

For some cues, preparatory cues such as streamers and punches or beeps are placed in front of the cue to guide the Foley artist's entrance (Figure 6.6). When recording with headphones, the 3-beep system is often used. A 1kHz tone is often used for the individual beeps; however, lower frequencies are equally effective and often more comfortable for the Foley artist. Each beep lasts a single frame and is spaced one second apart. An additional second of silence is added after the third beep to assist in the placement. Once created, a 3-beep clip can be saved with a session template and used for multiple cues.

Once a cue is recalled with a memory location, the mixer places the tail of the three beep at the header of the cue. If working with a pre-roll, set the length of the pre-roll to be slightly longer than the 3-beep clip.

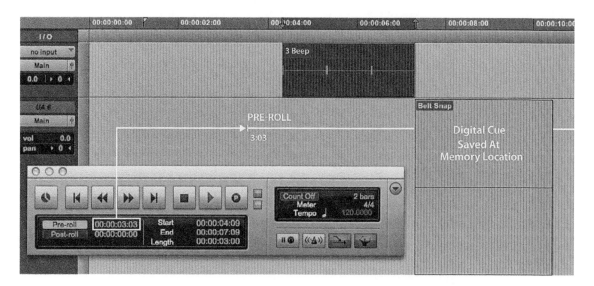

Figure 6.7 Digital Cue with Pre-Roll that Exceeds the 3-Beep

PLAYLISTING

Playlists are nested tracks within a track where alternate takes can be recorded, stored, and edited. Once recorded, entire clips or edited portions of a clip can be rated and promoted to the main playlist. Should the Foley mixer need to hear additional takes at a later date, he or she can open the playlist window and audition individual takes without having to move clips into place. The session is delivered to the mixer with the circled takes placed on the main playlist (Figure 6.8).

LOOPING

For short cues that are rhythmically complex, looping is an alternate approach to recording Foley. By looping the cue, the Foley artist can make immediate adjustments to the sync without having the take interrupted. When looping in Pro Tools, playlists and their respective clips are

Figure 6.8 Playlists Allow the Mixer to Nest Alternate Takes within the Same Track. Individual Takes Can Be Rated and Promoted to the Main Playlist (Circled Take)

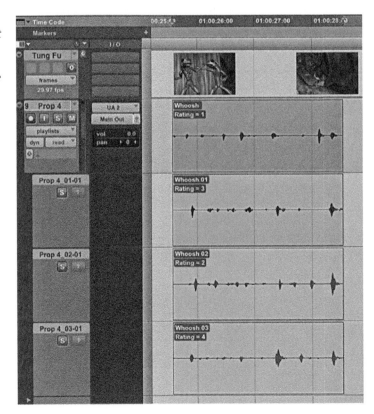

automatically generated, making it easy to select a take from individual passes. When loop recording, make sure the preparatory cues are included in the edit selection and that sufficient time is left at the end of each pass for the artist to re-set.

FOLEY EDITING

The lead or supervising Foley editor is responsible for cueing a session, cleaning up the audio, tightening sync, and preparing tracks for the mix. They attend the spotting session with the supervising sound editor and develop a full understanding of where and why Foley is needed. Once recorded, the editor's job is to clean the takes, removing extraneous sounds and additional material recorded in the take. In most cases the Foley artist will "land the cue" meaning that the sync is satisfactory. However, there are times when the performance is compelling yet the sync is slightly off. When this occurs, the Foley editor must decide if and how much editing should be used to tighten the sync. Like dialogue, footsteps and prop movements possess an internal rhythm that is best preserved when possible. This decision to edit is often contextual as sync is less critical when the sound plays in the background. Props are more likely to require sync adjustments as they often occur during well-defined sync points. Some scenes are so visually complex that you have to abandon sync and find a rhythm or composition that feels natural.

You can cut sync.
You can't cut feel.

Bob Rutledge
(*The Foley Grail*)

CHAPTER 7

THE PRODUCTION PATH

OVERVIEW

The production path is divided into three phases: *preproduction*, *production*, and *postproduction*. Workflows are developed for each production phase with the aim of optimizing the collective efforts of the production team. The saying "You can have it good, fast, or cheap, but you can only have two of the three" summarizes the forces that influence soundtrack development (Figure 7.1). In practice, "good" costs money, "fast" costs money, and too often there is "no" money. Of the three options, making it good is least negotiable. Therefore, the effective management of resources (time being the greatest) is key to the success of any animated film.

> If you fail to plan, you plan to fail.
>
> Don Bluth

Figure 7.1
Production Triangle

PREPRODUCTION

*To achieve great
things, two things
are needed; a plan,
and not enough
time.*

Leonard Bernstein

OVERVIEW

Preproduction is the planning and design phase where the story is refined and project logistics are worked out. First time directors are often unsure at what point sound designers and composer are brought into the process. Storyboarding session are an effective opportunity to introduce the supervising sound editor and composer to the project (Figure 7.2). When storyboarding, the animation team acts out individual shots, speaking dialogue in character, and mouthing SFX and humming music. These sessions are often more insightful than the spotting sessions that occur in postproduction. In addition, they provide the sound team with opportunities for creative input, expanding the director's options as they refine each shot or scene. Through this process, the supervising sound editor and composer develop a budget and production schedule that is integrated into the master budget and schedule.

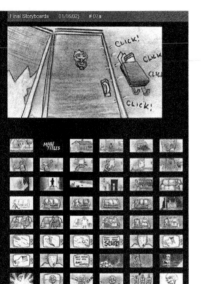

Figure 7.2 *Storyboard for* Trip to Granny's *(2001)*

ENLISTING A SOUND CREW

The animation process is at its best when a creative community of collaborators is assembled to work on a project governed by a shared vision. The enlisting of a sound crew can be a daunting task for animators less familiar with sound production. For small independent projects, financial compensation is often limited, and directors must promote intrinsic benefits when enlisting a sound crew. These intrinsic rewards include networking with a community of filmmakers, the opportunity to further develop their specific skill sets, and the opportunity to be associated with a potentially successful film. Directors, new to the process, may be tempted to offer creative license as an additional enticement. However, experienced sound designers and composers prefer that the director be "appropriately" involved in all phases of the soundtrack development. Their time and creative efforts are optimized when the director articulates a clear vision for the soundtrack. When pitching a project, storyboards, scripts, and concept art are often effective tools to

*Imagination makes
communities.*

Robert Hass

generate interest. There are three primary individuals that the animator must enlist to develop a soundtrack. These include the supervising sound editor, the composer, and the re-recording mixer. The supervising sound editor will recruit and head the sound department that develops the dialogue and SFX assets. The composer works independently from sound editorial, heading up a team of music editors, music supervisors, and musicians to produce the score. The re-recording mixer(s) will receive dialogue, music, and FX tracks and shape them into a cohesive mix. There are many supporting roles in each of these departments that were outlined in earlier chapters. If each of the primary roles are properly staffed, the remaining hierarchy will follow and clear lines of communication and workflow will be established.

DEVELOPING A SOUNDTRACK BUDGET

Two elements grow smaller as the production progresses: *budgets* and *schedules*. It is important to define these factors and tie them in with any expectations for soundtrack development. Input from the sound designer and composer is critical when developing a budget for audio production, especially in avoiding hidden costs. The sound crew can provide accurate cost estimates and negotiate directly with vendors. Table 7.1 gives a listing of possible expenses incurred in the production of a soundtrack.

PROJECT MANAGEMENT

The animation process involves a multitude of technologies and workflows that must work in tandem. One means of managing an animation project is through the use of a *production website* (Figure 7.3). There the production team can access concept art, a production calendar, a message board, e-mail links, and a partitioned drive for asset sharing. The production calendar is an important means of sequencing tasks, setting deadlines, and organizing meeting times. Many calendar programs can send automated reminders to the production crew. Most of the media associated with animation is too large to send via email. Presently, there are numerous web-based FTP *(file transfer protocol)* sites that facilitate file storage and sharing over the Internet. FTP is a client/server protocol that allows clients to log in to a remote server, browse the directories in the server, and upload (send) or download (retrieve) files from the site. As with calendar programs, some FTP sites send automatic messages to the client when new content is added.

Table 7.1 Budget Consideration for Soundtrack Development

Principal Dialogue, Voice-Over, and ADR	Compare SAG (Screen Actors Guild) rates and online sources when developing an estimate for voice talent. Also consider potential studio rental, equipment rental, and engineering fees, which vary by location.
Foley	Most Foley props are acquired as cheaply as possible from garage sales and dumpster diving. In some locations, prop rental companies provide a wide range of hard-to-find props at reasonable rates. There will be additional costs associated with studio rental, the Foley mixer, and the Foley artists.
SFX Libraries	Individual SFX can be purchased for specific needs. If a specific library is required, budget approximately $125 per CD.
Production Music Cues	Music Licensing. Production libraries are usually more reasonable than copy-protected music that has been commercially released. Licensing fees for small independent projects currently range from $100 to $300 dollars a cue.
Synchronization, Master, and Videogram License	These fees are negotiated with the copyright holder. Clearly define the nature of your request to negotiate the lowest fees. Many publishers are licensing songs at no charge for projects, hoping to receive performance royalties instead.
Composer or Creative Fees	These fees vary by composer. A creative fee only covers the writing of the cues. Additional cost can occur in producing the cues.
Sound Editors	Check the sound editors guild for a current rate guide for union editors. Also check with area recording studios for local mix/editor rates. https://www.editorsguild.com/Wages.cfm
Rental Fees	Most sound equipment needed for an animation production can be rented. Even plug-ins are now available for rental. The decision to rent or buy often comes down to availability and production schedules.
Backup Drives	It is important to backup your work with at least one level of redundancy. Drives are a cost effective means of securing your media assets.

PRODUCTION STANDARDS

A critical and often overlooked aspect of project management is the establishment of production standards. These standards are established in preproduction to facilitate the interchange of media files and to promote synchronization. When properly adhered to, production standards eliminate the need for unnecessary file conversion or transcoding that can potentially degrade the media files. Table 7.2 gives a list of production standards associated with standard definition video. Individual parameters will vary with specific release formats, software requirements, and variations in workflow.

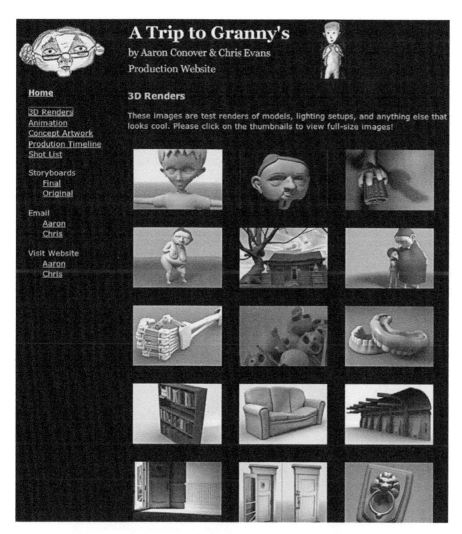

Figure 7.3 A Production Website Features Many of the Collaborative Tools Useful for the Production of Animation

The sound designer and composer will use the time code displayed in the burn-in window to set their session start timing to match (Figure 7.4). The burn-in is also useful to check for monitor latency that can result from converting digital video to NTSC for ADR and Foley sessions. Even though the animation is done at 24 fps, each render to the sound designer should be at 29.97 if releasing in standard definition NTSC. The work print should provide sufficient video resolution while not monopolizing the edit or mix windows.

Table 7.2 Audio Standards for Standard Definition Projects

Production Variables	Industry Standard for NTSC
Sample Rate	48 kHz (minimum)
Bit Depth(s)	16 or 24 bit (24 recommended prior to encoding)
File Type(s)	BWF, Aiff, MXF, mp3, AAC
Video Wrapper	QuickTime or WMP
Video Codec's	QuickTime, H.264, DV 25 MXF
Video Frame Speed	29.97fps (Once Imported, Pro Tools Frame Speed is fixed and cannot change)
Video size and resolution	No Standard (check with Supervising Sound Editor and Re-Recording Mixer)
Time code start time for burn in	No Standard (stay consistent throughout production)

Figure 7.4 The Burn-in Window Indicates the Current Timecode of the Film in Progress. The Larger Time Code Window Indicates a Typical Session Start Time Set in the DAW

RELEASE FORMATS

One of the initial decisions made prior to mixing a media project is determining the *release format(s)*. Audio resolution, dynamic range, and available channels vary from format to format. Establishing the project's release format(s) is an important step toward focusing soundtrack workflow and mix. Today there are a multitude of release formats to consider including theatrical, festival, consumer, online, and personal devices. Theatrical soundtracks are produced and exhibited under the most optimal conditions. The specifications for festival screenings are similar but continue to favor stereo mixes over multi-channel mixes. Consumer formats such as DVD and BluRay can deliver multi-channel audio at high resolutions. Online deliver has become the dominant mode of distribution with QuickTime, Vimeo, YouTube, and iTunes heading the list. Steady improvements in the codecs employed by these online delivery systems have led to increases in quality, limited only by the consumer's choice of monitors. Tables 7.3 and 7.4 give a listing of release

Table 7.3 Audio Specifications for Theatrical and Home Theater Release Formats

Release Formats	Channels	Codec(s)	Resolution	Data Rates
DV-Tape (Festivals)	2–4	PCM	48 kHz/16 bit	Not Applicable
Film and DVD	5.1	AC-3 (Dolby) DTS	48 kHz/24 bit	448 mbps (AC-3) 1.5 Mbps (DTS)
BluRay	5.1–13.1	Dolby Digital Plus (AC-3) Dolby True HD (MLP) DTS HD (Master Audio)	192 kHz/24 bit	6.1 Mbps (AC-3) 18 Mbps (MLP) 6 Mbps (DTS HD)

Table 7.4 Audio Specifications for Computer/Internet Release Formats

Players	Channels	Codec(s)	Resolution	Data Rates
QuickTime	2–Multi	WAV, AIFF, Apple Lossless, AAC, Mp3	Up to 192 kHz/24 bit	Up to 320 kbps
Flash (web)	Stereo	mp3, AAC	22.050 and 44.1 kHz	Not Provided
YouTube	2–Multi	mp3, AAC, Vorbis	44.1 kHz	192 kbps
Vimeo	2–Multi	AAC	44.1 kHz	320 kbps
iTunes	2–Multi	WAV, AIFF, Apple Lossless, mp3, AAC	Up to 96 kHz	Up to 320 kbps

*Note that higher data rates require higher bandwidth.

formats and their current audio specifications. These specifications are constantly evolving so it is important to research these options prior to establishing production standards.

PRODUCTION

OVERVIEW

The production time required to produce each minute of animation is significantly longer than that of live action. This extended schedule can work to the advantage of the sound crew, providing time for ideas to germinate. Though the focus in production is primarily on visuals, there are opportune moments for soundtrack development as well. During the production phase, motion tests are made and multiple versions of the animatic are generated. Motion tests provide an opportunity for sound designers to test their initial design concepts for moving objects. As each new animatic is generated, progressively more detailed movements, gestures, timings, backgrounds, and props are revealed. These added details could be used to refine the temp FX and music. At later stages in production, the animatic is a nearly completed version of the film. Many aspects of the temp effect can be used in the final, blurring the line between production and postproduction.

CREATING TEMP TRACKS

Animatics are assembled from storyboards, creating a format where temp FX, music, and scratch dialogue are initially cut. Temp tracks can serve as an important reference for picture editors developing the timings of a track. The animatic is also an important means for script development as the scratch dialogue is evaluated during this stage. It is important (at this stage) to identify any copy-protected music that may influence the animation process (pre-score). By identifying these cues in advance, the music supervisor creates lead-time needed to secure the licensing before the production schedule begins. The *2D animatic* is the first and most basic work print consisting of still images that are imported from the storyboard. These stills are gradually replaced with rough animation and preliminary camera work to produce a *pre-visualization* work print. For the sound designer new to animation, early versions of the animatic can be a bit of a shock. Boxy looking characters float across the floor, arms stretched out and sporting blank facial expressions. This print can be used for *initial screenings* to demonstrate the soundtrack to the director or test audiences. When the basic animation has been completed, *timings* are *locked* and a *temporary work print* is produced. The final stage of animation production includes compositing, lighting, special effects, rendering, and end-titles. A title sequence (if used) is added at this point in preparation for picture lock. When these elements are combined, the *final work print* is generated and the postproduction phase begins.

PRODUCTION TASKS FOR THE SOUND AND MUSIC DEPARTMENTS

Just as the animatic is a work in progress, so too are the temp tracks. Preliminary work at the production stage promotes creativity, organization, and acquisition. However, it is important to be flexible during production as the timings are still evolving. Animation studios have long recognized the benefits of researching the subject matter in the field; this approach can extend to audio research as well. Designers can explore the physics of how objects move, gain insight into the specific props needed, and experiment with various design approaches. Composers can develop initial themes based on the research of period, ethnic, or stylistic music. The production phase is an ideal time to acquire a specialized SFX library for the project. This library can be developed with original recordings or acquiring commercially. Any work completed during the production phase may potentially be included in the final soundtrack, blurring the distinction between production and postproduction.

> If you don't show up for work on Saturday, don't bother coming in on Sunday.
>
> Jeffrey Katzenberg

POSTPRODUCTION

OVERVIEW

In live action "picture lock" signals the beginning of the formal postproduction phase. In animation, the timing of the animatic is set much earlier, blurring the point in which production ends and postproduction begins. During the spotting session, the director screens the film with the composer and supervising sound editor to map out the specific needs for the soundtrack. At this point, the supervising sound editor may bring on additional crew to meet the remaining production deadlines. Nearly all scoring takes place in post as music cues are timed closely to the picture. Where the production phase is a time to explore ideas, the postproduction phase is the time to commit.

> If it weren't for the last minute, nothing would get done.
>
> Anonymous

PICTURE LOCK

Picture lock, or "picture latch" as it is known in sound departments, is an important concept that warrants procedural discussions between the animators and sound editorial. Re-edits of a film are a normal part of the process and both the sound and music departments must be prepared to deal with additional picture changes. However, the setbacks caused by additional picture edits can be minimized if the animator provides an *EDL* (Edit Decision List) or *Change List* documenting each change. These lists document the timings of individual edits, and the order in which they were made. Each picture edit is mirrored in the audio editing program. Once the edits are completed, additional audio editing is required to smooth the newly created edit seams. The score is typically most impacted by re-edits due to its linear nature. It is important for the animator to at least consider the possibility that the soundtrack can also be an effective means of developing or fixing a shot that is not working. Picture edits, when improperly handled, slow down the production, rob the designers of creative time, and place a strain on the relationships of the entire production team.

POSTPRODUCTION TASKS FOR THE SOUND AND MUSIC DEPARTMENTS

As the animation process nears completion, *compositing* and *effects animation* provide additional visual detail that informs the sound design. Table 7.5 shows tasks associated with the postproduction phase.

Table 7.5 *Tasks for Postproduction*

ADR (Automated Dialog Replacement) and Additional Voice-Over.	There are several reasons to record additional Voice-Over and ADR near the final stage of the production. These include . . . 1. Changes to the script. 2. Availability of new voice talent. 3. The potential for a better interpretation resulting from the increased visual detail available near the final stage. 4. The development of foreign language versions.
Scoring	A spotting session for score occurs immediately after the picture is locked. After that point, individual cues are written or edited from commercial libraries.
Foley	Foley is recorded to provide footsteps, prop, and cloth performances.
Creating Design Elements	At this stage, characters, objects, and environments are fully flushed out in both appearance and movement. Design elements are created to represent the characters, objects, and environments that are too specific or imaginative to cut from a library.
Sound Editorial	Sound editors clean up tracks, tighten sync, re-conform picture edits, and organize tracks for delivery to the mix stage.
Mixing	Mixing is the final process in soundtrack development. This process varies considerably based on the track count and length of the film. The director, supervising sound editor, and music editor should attend the final mix to insure that each stem is properly represented.
Layback	Once the mix is completed, the printmaster is delivered to the picture editor for layback. During the layback, the mixer and director screen the film for quality control, checking for level and sync issues.

CHAPTER 8

SOUND EDITING

OVERVIEW

A sound editor is called upon to complete a multitude of tasks including designing, syncing, and organizing audio clips and tracks. Many of the seemingly routine editing tasks can become creative opportunities when approached with a design mindset. Editors learn to prioritize tasks, working quickly on some tasks to create time for more complex edits. There are many software applications and associated plug-ins designed for media production. Pro Tools is one such application and is fully representative of the tools required for completing a soundtrack. Regardless of the specific technologies used, the goal of sound editing is to support story telling. Thus, editing is most effective when transparent to the narrative process. This transparency is why sound editing is referred to as the invisible art.

SYNCING SOUND TO PICTURE

Editors are routinely called on to cut sound to picture in sync. In most cases, this means aligning the header of a clip to a specific frame or time code location. Often, additional adjustments to the initial placement are needed to tighten/slip the sync or re-conform to a new picture edit. This can be accomplished by nudging by frame, snapping to position using keyboard shortcuts, or spotting to time code. When the sync point occurs within the clip, that specific location is marked, providing the editor with a spotting reference (Figure 8.1). The clip is aligned to the sync point rather than the clip header. The editor must then determine how best to approach and exit the sync point. This technique is referred to as *backtiming*.

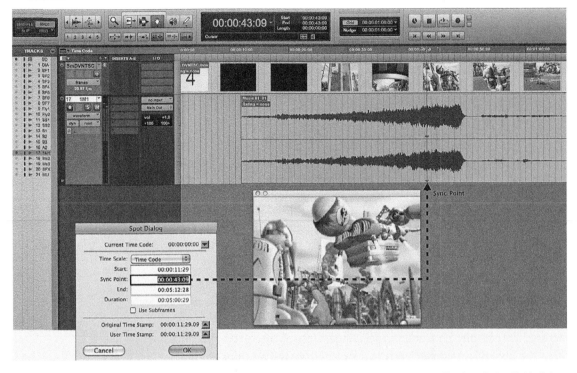

Figure 8.1 Clip Marked with a Sync Point Indicating where the Score Reaches a Climatic Point. The Sync Point Field of the Spot Dialog Box is Highlighted, Indicating that its Current Value Will Be Applied to the Music Cue

TRIMMING AND CUTTING

Whether the goal is to adjust the length of a clip or remove unwanted sound, trimming and cutting are two of the most basic edits performed by sound editors. The *trim* tool is used for reducing or extending the length of a clip from the header and tail (Figure 8.2). Lengthening is only possible if hidden material *(handle)* already exists.

Figure 8.2 In this Example, the Trim Tool Is Being Used to Pull out Existing Handle from the Header of the Clip

Cutting differs from trimming in that it removes sound from a specified edit selection rather than adjusting length (Figure 8.3). Some editors substitute the delete key for the cut command, though, unlike the delete key, the cut command creates break points that preserve the underlying automation that exists before and after the edit.

Intercuts are applied to edit selections within a clip. Intercuts are a common technique used by music editors to conform songs and production music to specified lengths (Figure 8.4). Intercuts reduce the length of a cue while preserving the song introductions and endings. Intercuts are typically performed in shuffle mode, allowing the remaining clips to snap together once the intercut is made. Several musical factors must be considered when performing an intercut, including lyrics, form, tempo, instrumentation, and key signature.

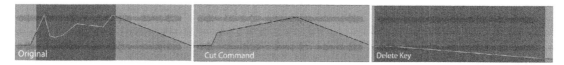

Figure 8.3 In these Examples, the Volume Graph of an Edit Selection Changes Based on the Use of the Cut Command Verses the Delete Key

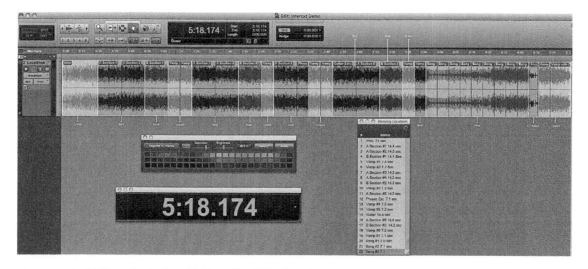

Figure 8.4 In this Example, the B-52 Hit "Love Shack" Has Been Separated into 33 Individual Clips to Facilitate Intercutting

Customized

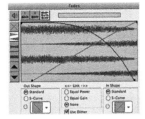

Preset

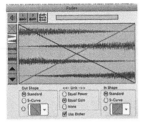

Figure 8.5 By Selecting None as the Fade Option, the Editor Can Move the In and Out Points of the Fades to Specified Locations and Design Individual Fade Curves for the Fade In and Outs

FADES

Fades are commonly applied to the head and tail of clips to eliminate the sonic ticks or pops that occur when the audio is not trimmed at the zero crossing. Cross-fades are applied to edit seams to smooth out differences in volume levels that often occur. They are useful when compositing, intercutting, or looping clips. Pre-set fades are fast and easy, but for highly exposed edits, customized fades will often produce a more transparent transition across the edit seam (Figure 8.5).

COMPOSITING TAKES

Compositing is a technique where a single take is assembled using selected portions of alternate takes (Figure 8.6). One of the first tasks in compositing is to develop a unique set of criteria for rating takes. The play listing feature in Pro Tools greatly facilitates this process, allowing the editor to view, audition, cut, and promote all related takes within the same playlist. Fades are then added to the new edit seams and the composite track is auditioned to determine if the edits work in context.

RING-OUTS

Abrupt edits can be smoothed by adding reverb just prior to the tail of an audio clip, effectively extending the clip length in proportion to the reverb decay time. Editors use this technique to create *ring-outs* for dialogue, FX, and music. This technique is most effective if reverb is introduced late enough that it will not draw attention, but early enough to generate sufficient energy to sustain beyond the edit point. Ring-outs are created by automating the wet/dry ratio on the reverb plug-in (Figure 8.7). Dialogue ring-outs are common near picture edits that represent a jump in time. For example, screams or sinister laughter are made to postlap into the following scene for emphasis. When working with production music libraries or source music, it is often necessary to make an abrupt edit for timing purposes.

Ring-outs smooth music edits, making the termination point of the cue sound natural.

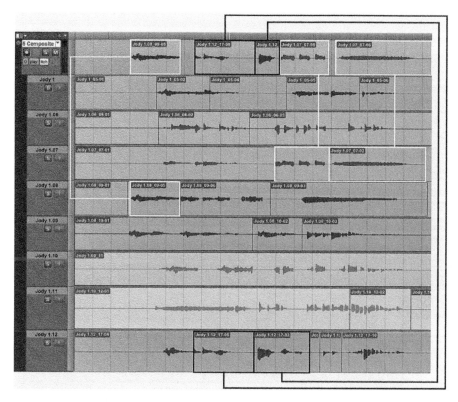

Figure 8.6 *In the Playlist View Shown, Alternate Takes Can Be Displayed, Auditioned, and Separated while Showing the Composite Track*

TIME-SCALING

Time-scaling or Time Compression/Expansion (TC/E) involves changing the clip length without losing any of the original material. Time-scaling is accomplished by adding or subtracting samples from an audio clip. This process can alter the pacing or tempo of a clip without affecting the underlying pitch. The percentage of TC/E that can be achieved while still maintaining sonic transparency (no audible artifacts) is dependent on the length of the file, type of material being processed, sample rate of the session, and the effectiveness of the algorithm. The following are typical scenarios where time-scaling techniques are useful.

a. To conform an existing clip to a specified length where no additional handle exists.

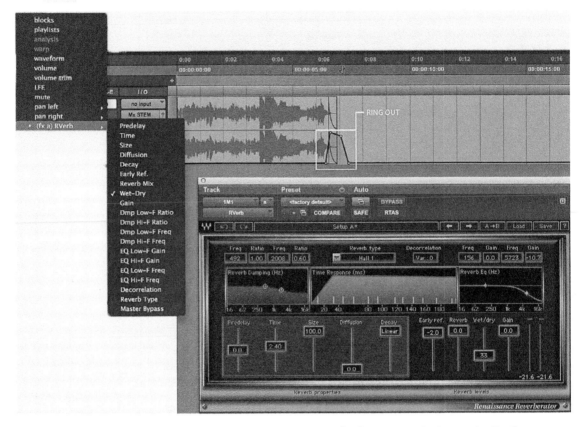

Figure 8.7 In the Screen Shot Shown, the Track View Selector Is Set For (fx a) RVerb with the Automation Playlist Displaying Wet/Dry Automation. Notice How Reverb Is Introduced near the End of the Clip

    b. To move transients within a clip without changing the clip's head or tail position. For example, tightening dialogue sync or making a specific point in a music cue hit to specific on-screen action.

    c. Speeding up the disclaimer dialogue for a TV commercial.

    d. Superimposing phrasing on a line of dialogue or a lyric.

Pro Tools has a time-scaling feature called elastic audio that is built into its application. The range warping feature is particularly useful for tightening sync or making a cue hit precisely on the action (Figure 8.8). Vocalign (discussed in Chapter 3) is an industry standard for tightening dialogue sync and superimposing phrasing.

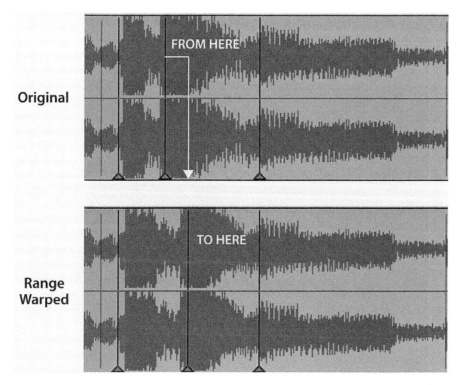

Figure 8.8 *Notice How the Middle Warp Marker Has Moved to the Center of the Left and Right Markers. None of the Audio Before or After the Outside Markers Are Altered*

PITCH SHIFTING

Pitch shifting is one of the primary means of creating variation in repetitive sounds. It can be applied to a clip to change a subject's age, size, or gender. Pitch shifting can also be used to enhance our perception of speed. SFX can be pitch shifted to create harmonic or dissonance relationships with a music cue or SFX. Some pitch-shifting plug-ins split the signal to produce *harmonizing* effects. Harmonizing is an effective way to fatten sounds and give them additional emotional weight. In a subjective sense, minor 2nds, tri-tones, and major 7ths are intervals capable of producing tension. Minor 3rds and 6ths can promote a dark, sad, or foreboding feel. Perfect 4ths and 5ths are neutral, and major 3rds and 6ths are consonant. Sounds can be pitched by cents, semitones, or octaves. There are 100 cents for each semitone and 12 semitones per octave. Like TC/E, there are limits to the extent to which a signal can be pitched without producing audible artifacts.

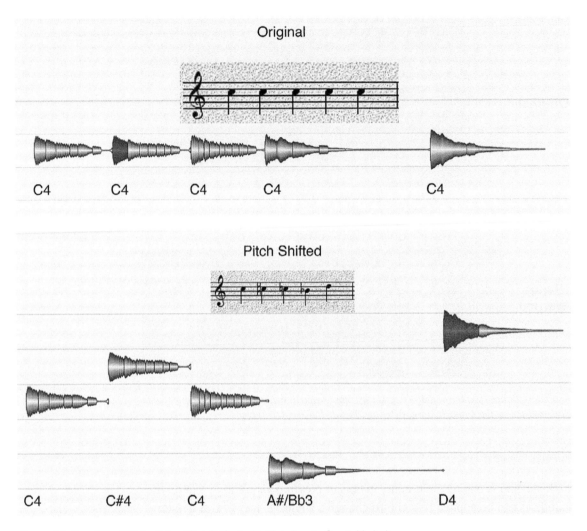

Figure 8.9 Repetitive SFX Are Being Pitch Shifted with Melodyne to Create Variation

It should be noted that pitch shifting is more transparent when processed in sessions of higher sample rates.

VARI-SPEED

Linking TC/E with pitch shifting processing results in a *vari-speed* effect. This digital technique emulates pitch and time characteristics associated with analog devices like tape decks and vinyl recordings. Vari-speed is used to create acceleration/de-acceleration effects for powered objects like engines or generators (Figure 8.10). The ability to customize the rate at which these objects power up or down is useful when matching on-screen movements or implying dynamic change. Vari-speed is also used to support comic misdirection. In this application, the sound of an object losing power becomes an analogy for the misdirection. Vari-speed effects are also used in narrative moments when a character transitions from fantasy to reality.

REVERSE AND REWIND

Reverse is an audio-suite or rendered process used by editors for a variety of creative applications such as designed languages, terminating effects, and

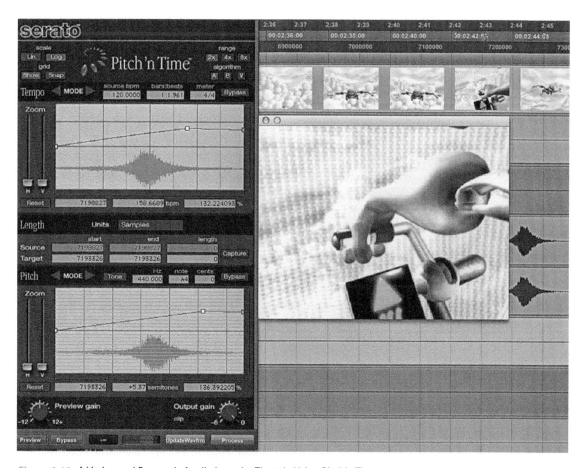

Figure 8.10 A Vari-speed Process Is Applied to a Jet Throttle Using Pitch'n Time

transitional sounds. For example, the terminating sound of a sci-fi door closing is achieved by reversing compressed air. Whooshes are often reversed and used to support transitional moments or shots where the visuals are also rewound. The *pre-verb* effect used in horror films is created by reversing dialogue, adding reverb, and re-reversing the dialogue. When played back, we hear the reversed reverb just prior to the dialogue. Rewind is a reverse effect produced by scrubbing the audio backwards in time. This effect is often used in scenes where the image plays back in reverse, usually indicating a time shift in the narrative. Capturing a rewind effect requires the outputting of the DAW signal to an additional recording device and importing the captured sound back into the session.

SOUND REPLACEMENT

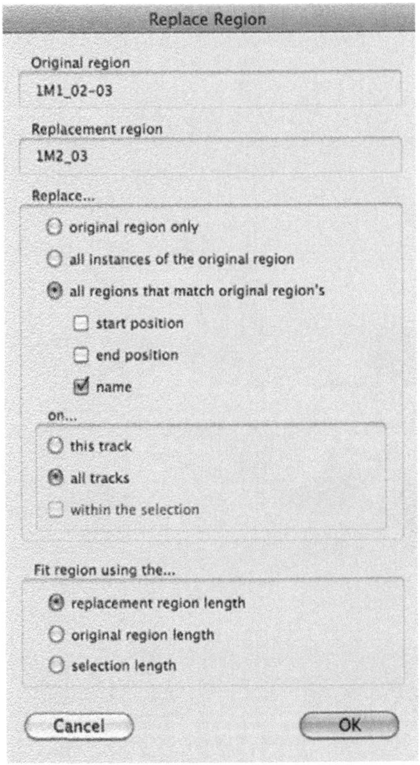

Replace Region

Original region

1M1_02-03

Replacement region

1M2_03

Replace...

○ original region only
○ all instances of the original region
◉ all regions that match original region's
  ☐ start position
  ☐ end position
  ☑ name

on...

○ this track
◉ all tracks
☐ within the selection

Fit region using the...

◉ replacement region length
○ original region length
○ selection length

Cancel   OK

Figure 8.11 Sound Replacement Software Provides a Variety of Options for Batch Replacement

Requests to substitute one sound for another are a common occurrence in sound editing. If multiple versions of a sound already exist, sound replacement can become time consuming. Most audio editing programs have sound replacement functionality built within or achieve replacement with plug-ins (Figure 8.11). Sound replacement parameters can be configured to work at the track or session level. Once the clips are replaced, the editor must revisit each clip to insure that no additional editing is required.

NOISE REDUCTION

Noise reduction is often needed to clean up tracks before they are sent to the final mix. This is especially true for field recordings that were captured under less than ideal conditions. Equalizers, gates, and specialized noise reduction plug-ins are essential tools for cleaning up tracks. Equalizers approach noise reduction from the frequency domain. They can be used to roll-off noise that occurs above and below a desired signal, or they can be used to filter a selected range of frequencies that might mask a given signal. Peak filters are like sonic erasures; some are wider and impact a larger portion of the signal while some are more narrow and discrete. The control that adjusts the width of frequency impacted by an equalizer is referred to as the Q. Gates and expanders approach noise reduction from the amplitude domain. The better the signal-to-noise ratio, the more effective they become. Gates and expanders operate by setting a threshold for amplitude. Any signal that drops below the threshold is effectively muted. Noise reduction is most transparent when multiple approaches are used. Thus, noise reduction software often incorporates both EQ and Expansion/Gating. Noise reduction plug-ins can manipulate a multitude of narrow frequency bands or notch filters to achieve substantial reduction of unwanted noise while preserving the intended signal.

SIDE-CHAIN GATE

Sounds are often given greater weight when layered with additional sounds. When this approach involves multiple iterations of the sound, side-chain gating becomes a practical alternative to multiple edits. As discussed earlier, the gate is a signal processor that uses amplitude thresholds to determine whether a sound will play or be muted (gated). One common application to side-chain gating is to create a secondary track that hosts a constant signal (typically low frequency). The gate is placed on the secondary track but receives its input (key) from the primary track. When the sound on the primary track exceeds the threshold (like a gun going off), the gate opens and the secondary track is un-muted. When the primary tracks signal falls below the threshold, the secondary track returns to its muted state, effectively automating cuts.

FUTZING

Futzing involves the digital processing of a signal to imply that it is transmitting from a specific playback device. Futzing is also used to transition a cue from source to underscore or to move from an exterior shot to an interior shot. One of the key elements of futzing is bandwidth limiting. Bandwidth limiting involves the paired use of low and high-pass filters to create a narrow frequency response associated with many playback devices (Figure 8.12).

Televisions, radios, phones, and public address system are commonly futzed to imply source or diegesis. A good example of futzing can be heard in the scene

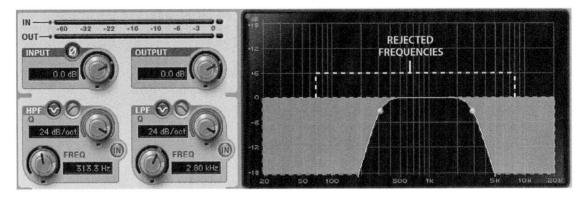

Figure 8.12 *The Portion that Is Grayed Out Represents Frequency Content in a Signal that Has Been Eliminated*

from *Iron Giant* (1999) where Eli and his mother converse by phone. In this scene, Mrs. Hughes' voice is futzed only when she is off-screen. For additional realism, the sound editor included futzed BGs in Eli's phone, representing the diner where his mother was working. Futzing is not limited to frequency bandwidth limiting. Third party plug-ins like Speakerphone (Figure 8.13) and Futzbox provide the sound editor with additional futzing parameters. These include physical modeling of devices and spaces and the addition of sonic artifacts such as radio squelch, vinyl ticks, and pitch warping. One advantage to using futzing plug-ins is that all of the parameters can be automated to transition from source to underscore or vice versa.

Figure 8.13 *Speakerphone Applied to the Source Music*

DOPPLER

The Doppler effect combines pitch variation with volume and panning to enhance the sound of an object as it passes. This perceptual phenomenon reflects the perspective (point of view) of an observer in relation to a moving object (Figure 8.14). As an object approaches, it travels into its own sound waves, compressing them and causing the observer to perceive a rise in pitch. The opposite occurs as the object moves away. Many SFX are recorded with Doppler, oftentimes making more work for the editor as they attempt to match the clip to the picture. Doppler plug-ins allow the editor to take a static version of a sound and customize the pitch variation, volume, and panning to match the on-screen movements with exacting levels of realism. Doppler is frequently added to vehicles that pass or fly by a character. They are also added to whoosh effects to give them additional motion. The GRM Doppler plug-in can also generate circular or rotating effects such as tornadoes, helicopter blades, or twirling particles radiating from an explosion.

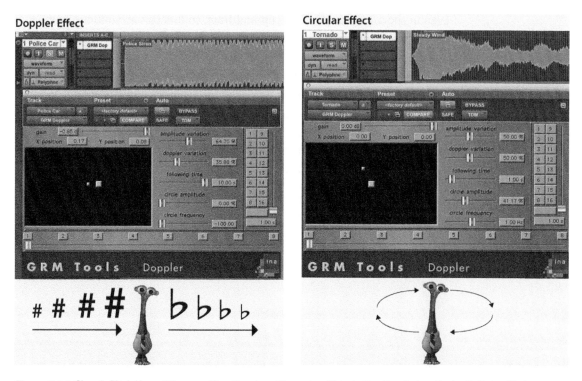

Figure 8.14 Signals Pitch Up and Down as They Pass by a Character. Objects Can Also Rotate Sonically Using Circle Amplitude and Frequency Controls

LOOPING

In some cases it is necessary to extend the length of the clip beyond the range in which time-compression tools are practical or transparent. In these situations, the sound editor may opt to extend the audio by means of looping. Music editors use looping to vamp a selection within a cue to meet certain length requirements. When looping musical material, it is important that the loop point match rhythmically, harmonically, and dynamically. If lyrics or a melodic line is involved, care should be taken to observe the line. FX editors commonly loop BGs for extended scenes. When looping BGs, the editor should avoid using portions of a clip that contain spikes or patterns that might advertise the loop. Most DAWs have a batch-fading feature that allows the editor to customize and apply a cross fade at the edit seam of each loop.

PREPARING TRACKS FOR DELIVERY TO THE MIX

Even in short form animation, clip and track counts can accumulate and become overwhelming if not properly managed. Tracks and clips should be ordered and labeled in a clear and logical manner so as not to confuse or create additional work for the mixer. Any unused tracks, plug-ins, or busses should be removed to optimize the system's resources and storage requirements. If a unique plug-in was used, duplicate the track and render the effect, providing the mixer with both a processed and unprocessed version in the event that the particular plug-in is not available on the mix stage. Sessions must be properly archived and labeled to insure that all assets are present.

CHAPTER 9

THE FINAL MIX

OVERVIEW

The Warner Brothers animated short *Rhapsody in Rivets* (1941) created an analogy between the construction of a building and the performance of a symphony (Figure 9.1). This analogy can be extended to the mixing of a soundtrack as well. The conductor for the mix is the film's director, responsible for articulating a vision that guides the performance. Sound *elements* are the individual instruments of the soundtrack. Just as related instruments meet in sectionals to work on timing, balance, and blend, similar elements are combined in a process known as *pre-dubbing*. Sectionals are followed by a dress rehearsal where all of the instruments are brought together and placed (panned) in their respective string, woodwind, brass, or percussion sections. The dress rehearsal for a film mix is the point in which pre-dubs are combined to create the dialogue, music, and FX *stems*. During this stage, the director works to balance (level) the individual parts measure by measure (frame by frame). In film mixing, the final concert is performed by the *re-recording mixer*. Like the concert pianist, the re-recording mixers have a multitude of keys (faders and knobs on a large console) from which they perform with expressive control over individual entrances, dynamics, and articulations (Figure 9.2). Finally, all of the players are assembled in a performance space, and like the concert hall, the mixers select spaces for each of the movements (scenes) in their cinematic symphony.

THE RE-RECORDING MIXER(S)

It is easy to step onto a mix stage and develop an impression that mixing is primarily technical in nature. However, in reality mixing is driven primarily by creativity, problem solving, and a strong aesthetic foundation for narrative film. It is true that mixers have a great deal of technology at their fingertips; however, they must become masters of that technology if it is to become

> If it sounds good, it is good.
>
> Duke Ellington

Figure 9.1 Rhapsody in Rivets

transparent to the mixing process. Mixers are responsible for developing pre-dubs, building stems, and recording the printmaster. They are also involved with mastering and encoding the audio for various release formats. They shape a multitude of tracks created by the sound and music departments into a cohesive soundtrack that is integral to the storytelling process. They use faders and panners to focus the scene and control its intensity. They strive to understand the narrative implications of every subtle adjustment; smoothing transitions between edits or scenes, defining spaces, and developing continuity. Mixers accomplish this by being sensitive to the narrative qualities of the film and the vision of the director. Mixers work collaboratively with directors, sound editors, and other mixers. They must be able to work for long periods of time under incredible pressure while maintaining a high level of diplomacy.

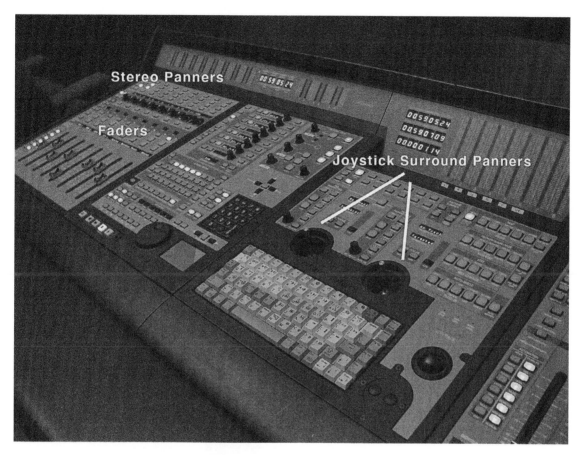

Figure 9.2 Mixing Console with Stereo and 5.1 Panners

SPEAKER CALIBRATION

When mixing a media project, it is important to differentiate *mix levels* from *monitoring levels*. Mix levels are created by adjusting individual track levels to produce inter-level differences. The changes made to individual track levels are reflected in the respective track output meters. These peak levels indicate the relative strength of the signal being sent to the monitors (speakers).

Monitor levels refer to amount of sound pressure level (SPL) created when the mix is played through a set of speakers. Consequently, a project mixed at high levels but monitored at low levels will sound dull and lifeless. Conversely, a project mixed at low levels but monitored at high levels may sound bright and noisy. To insure that a theatrical film mix will properly translate beyond the mix stage, *reference levels* have been established to guide the mixing process. Before mix levels can be properly set, monitor levels need to be *calibrated* to these reference levels. In film the most commonly accepted reference level is 85 dBspl (sound pressure levels in decibels) at −20 (Figure 9.3). When calibrating a speaker at this reference level, the engineer will play a reference tone (pink noise at −20) through each

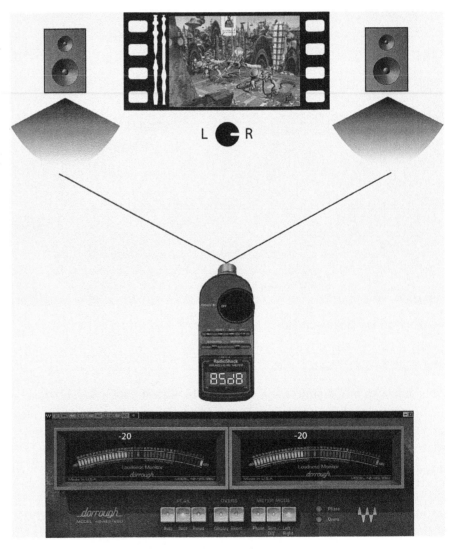

Figure 9.3 The Output Meters of a Master Fader at −20db Measuring 85dB on the SPL Meter. This is the Standard for Mixing a Theatrical Release in a Large Room

speaker, trimming the output of the speaker until it reads 85 dB on an SPL meter and -20 on the mix console meter. For television, the mix reference is often lowered to 79 dBspl, however, like the Internet and mobile applications, there currently are no standard reference levels.

DYNAMIC RANGE

Variations in dynamic range (soft to loud) contribute to the expressive quality of the film while also preventing the audience from becoming fatigued. Audiences perceive volume contextually. In other words, if a preceding scene is very soft and a loud sound is suddenly introduced, the audience will perceive it as being very loud. It is the context of changes in volume that audiences are most attuned to. Film mixers utilize approximately 40 dB of dynamic range in a theatrical mix (Figure 9.4). They pace dynamics to create interest through contrast rather than maximum volume. Figure 9.4 describes the optimum dynamic range for a theatrical presentation. Mixers for cinema can rely to a greater extent on a predictable playback system and environment. However, audiences are increasingly turning to the Internet and personal devices to acquire and experience media. This shift in delivery will require content providers to adopt new work flows and standards in an effort to create optimal mixes for these emerging formats.

> It's not how loud you make it, it's how you make it loud.
>
> Anonymous

CONFIGURING THE SESSION

If the sound editors have labeled and organized tracks and clips in a logical manner, the task of combining multiple sessions to create the master session will be greatly simplified. Some mixers color-code tracks by stem as a means of visually organizing a session, especially in mix view. Separating the video into shots or scenes provides a useful navigational map for the film (Figure 9.5). In addition, these regions can be used to define edit selections for static or snapshot automation. Memory locations and window configurations can be used to show or hide a variety of track configurations and display options.

PRE-DUBS

As a project grows in track count, there often comes a point where the number of tracks exceeds the practical limitations of a DAW or mix console.

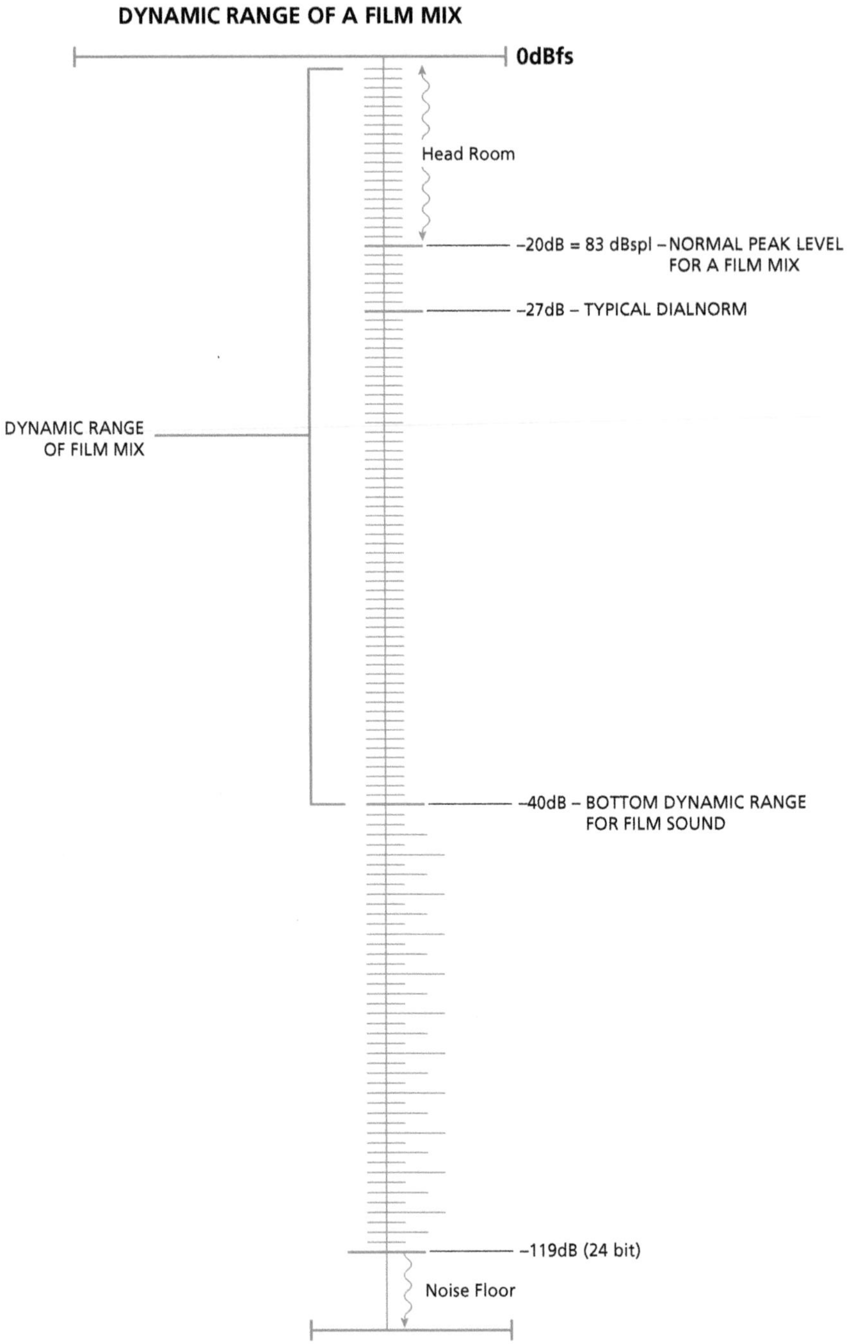

Figure 9.4 Dynamic Range of Theatrical Film Mix

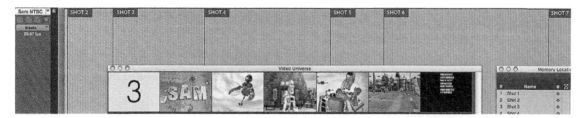

Figure 9.5 *The Video Track Shown is Separated by Shots to Facilitate Navigation and Signal Processing by shot*

Pre-dubbing is the process of combining tracks of similar type to facilitate the mix. During the pre-dubs, the mixer becomes familiar with individual tracks and looks for opportunities to combine related tracks. The following are some basic guidelines for pre-dubs:

- Combine elements that are part of a design element.
- Combine multiple elements if they are similar in character (i.e. gun handling, gun firing, gun shells).
- Combined multiple elements if they can share the same panning position.
- Combine multiple elements if they can share the same signal processing, especially reverb.

Mixers have the option of printing pre-dubs or creating virtual pre-dubs from tracks residing in the master session. One approach to creating virtual pre-dubs involves grouping like tracks and assigning them to a VCA or Voltage-Controlled Amplifier (Figure 9.6). With this approach, the group members are hidden unless they are needed for individual level or panning adjustments. A second approach involves bussing (pre-fade) like elements to an auxiliary track (Figure 9.7). This approach is preferable when signal processing is required and when it is necessary to meter the sum of the track outputs. Virtual pre-dubs have the advantage of being readily adjustable on the mix stage, eliminating the need to go off-line and re-import.

CREATING THE STEMS AND PRINTMASTER

The dialogue, music, and SFX elements are pre-dubbed separately. Each of the pre-dubs that will become a stem are leveled and panned in the context of the full mix to create the dialogue, music, and SFX stems. Reverb is added (if needed) at this stage, reinforcing the spaces or environments that appear

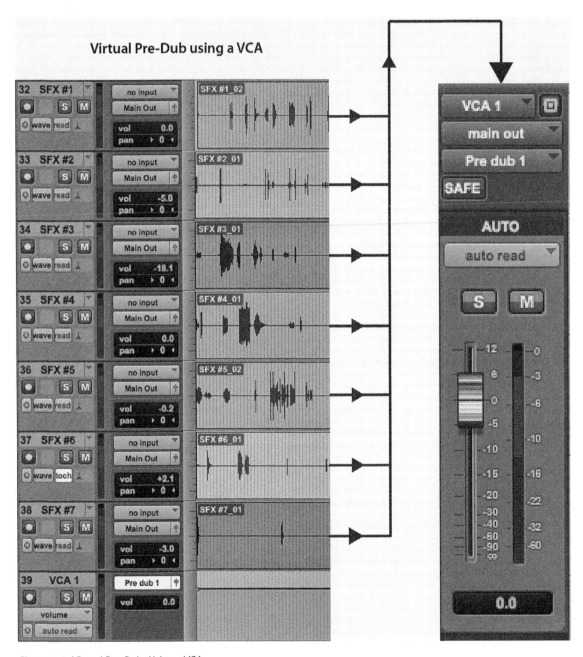

Figure 9.6 *Virtual Pre-Dubs Using a VCA*

Virtual Pre-Dub using an Aux Track

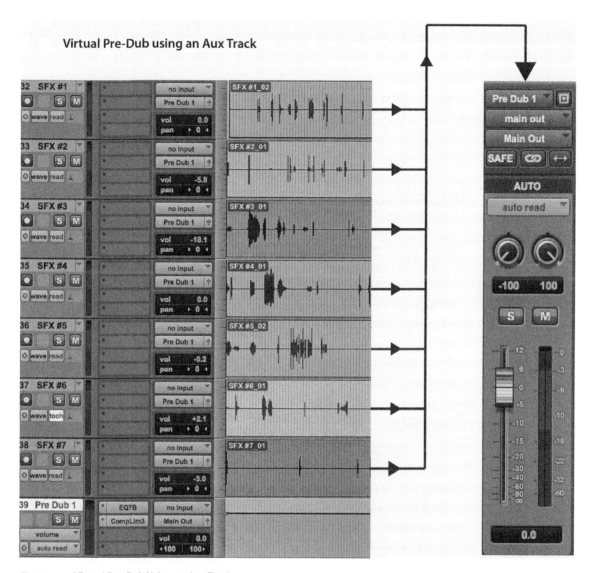

Figure 9.7 Virtual Pre-Dub Using an Aux Track

on-screen. Directors attend the mix at this stage to provide input and feedback as the mix progresses. In many cases, the dialogue, music, and FX editors are also on hand to perform any additional fixes that may be required. When building stems, the director and mixers are often faced with difficult choices regarding which sounds will play and how prominently they will be mixed. Dialogue, if present, will always take priority, consequently, much of the debate centers around the FX and music stems. Once these issues are resolved, the stems are combined to form the printmaster or complete soundtrack.

THE STEREO MIX

PANNING

The stereo mix is still the most common format for short form films. There are no specific rules for mixing but several panning conventions have emerged over the years. In most cases, principal dialogue is panned to the center, providing the most uniform coverage for the audience. Narration and Group ADR are often split out to the left and right channels to provide separation from the principal dialogue. Hard effects are panned to the position of their respective on-screen objects. Foley that is linked to dialogue (the cloth pass and footsteps) are panned to the center; otherwise Foley is panned to the on-screen position. Backgrounds or BGs are typically panned hard left and right, depending on the framing of the shot. Underscore is panned in stereo and source music is panned to the on-screen position as with hard effects.

LEVELING

Where panning establishes the horizontal placement for sounds, leveling creates the perception of depth. Leveling is the principal means of clarifying which elements in the soundtrack are most critical in supporting the narrative at any given moment. There are many approaches to setting levels for a mix. One approach to leveling is to set the initial level for each track at a low but audible level. The mix begins by leveling the dialogue tracks to establish the foreground and foundation of the mix. Cinematic dialogue is generally louder than conversational dialogue, perhaps as much as 10 additional dB. Therefore 76 to 79 dBspl is a good initial level, allowing for variations in dynamic range when applicable. Once the dialogue levels are set, supporting elements from the FX and music stem are brought up at levels that do not compete with the dialogue. If the dialogue begins to get lost in the mix, supportive elements are brought down before dialogue is brought up. Using this approach, leveling decisions become focused and purposeful and the mix will quickly develop.

SIGNAL PROCESSING

If the sound editors have been thorough in their work, very little corrective or sound shaping signal processing will be required at the mix stage. Signal processing is a broad and contextual topic deserving volumes of discussion. However, there are three processes that are universal to the mix process: reverb, EQ, and dynamic compression/limiting.

Reverb

Reverb is used to define the space where a given action is occurring. Reverb is processed in real time (RTAS) so that parameters can be adjusted as characters move through a variety of environments within a given scene. The primary controls for reverb include:

- Pre-Delay, the time interval between the direct sound and the first reflection.
- Time, determined by the rate the reverberant signal decays by 60 dB.
- Wet/Dry, the mix ratio between the dry (unprocessed) version and a wetted (processed) version.
- The Reverb Type, selectable algorithms that accurately mimic various spatial properties.

In addition to defining a space for principal dialogue and hard FX, a separate reverb is added to underscore and narration as a means of establishing their non-diegetic function.

Equalization (EQ)

The frequency range of human hearing can be divided up into 10 octaves, each contributing differently to our perception of the soundtrack as a whole. Re-recording mixers use EQ (equalization) to balance the frequency spectrum of a mix (Figure 9.8). EQ can also be used to pre-emphasize specific frequencies that will be most affected by the encoding process. Table 9.1 gives a breakdown of the 10 octaves and their specific contribution or affect on the mix.

Peak Limiting

Mixes can get very loud at times, approaching and exceeding full scale (clipping) when tracks are summed. To prevent clipping and the distortion

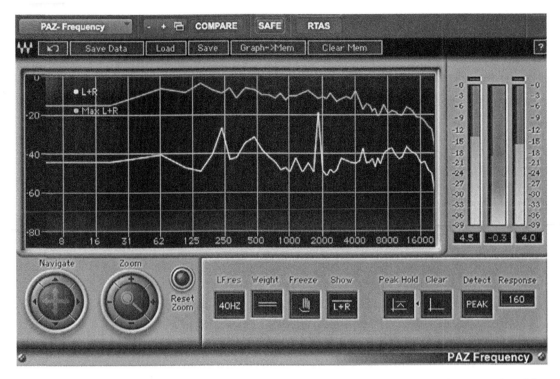

Figure 9.8 The Waves PAZ Frequency Analyzer Is Placed on the Master Fader to Create a Visual Representation of the Frequency Characteristics of an Entire Mix

that follows, a peak limiter is often placed on the master fader (Figure 9.9). Notice in the screenshot shown that both the ratio and threshold are extremely high (83.2:1 at -2.7 dB). When properly mixed, little or no signal will exceed the threshold of the limiter. However, having one in place provides a useful safety net.

THE MULTI-CHANNEL MIX

Multi-channel formats are standard for large budget theatrical releases and most video games. The multi-channel mix format expands the stereo field by adding a discrete center channel, a pair of surrounds (LsRs), and a LFE or low frequency effects channel (Figure 9.10). The most common format for multi-channel mixing is 5.1. The consumer or home theater layout for 5.1 places the left and right screen channels at roughly 30 degrees off axis from the center channel. The surrounds are angled at 110 degrees to

Table 9.1 *Characteristics of the 10 Octave Frequency Range*

1st Octave (20 Hz to 40 Hz). This octave is more heard than felt. Few speakers can reproduce these frequencies with adequate power. There is little musical content at this range. The LFE in a Dolby or DTS file starts at 20 Hz and extends to 120 Hz.

2nd Octave (40 Hz to 80 Hz). This octave is associated with the rumble of an LFE associated with SFX like earthquakes and the bottom end of an explosion. This octave can reduce the headroom in a mix without making it sound louder.

3rd Octave (80 Hz to 160 Hz). This is the octave where the lower end of the music score and SFX can be pushed with less risk of rumble.

4th Octave (160 Hz to 320 Hz). This octave is sometimes referred to as the mud-range when given too much level. However, this octave also contributes to the fullness of a mix when properly leveled.

5th Octave (320 Hz to 640 Hz). This is the lower portion of the mid-range where most of the dialogue, SFX, and Music compete for the foreground. Watch for masking of dialogue in this octave. When properly balanced, this octave can contribute to the subjective fullness and roundness to the mix. Our ears are most sensitive to the 5th and 6th octaves. Most playback devices are capable of reproducing these octaves accurately. Consequently, this component of the mix will effectively translate across multiple playback devices.

6th Octave (640 Hz to 1.28 kHz). Shares characteristics with the 5th octave. Excessive cuts and boosts in this range are responsible for nasal characteristics in the mix.

7th Octave (1.28 kHz to 2.56 kHz). This is the upper mid-range. Use this octave to add volume and definition to the 5th and 6th octaves. This is the bottom range for sibilance. Too much level at this range can create a harsh sounding mix that is fatiguing.

8th Octave (2.56 kHz to 5.12 kHz). This is the lower range of the treble portion of the mix. This octave is sometimes referred to as the presence range since boosting these frequencies brings out the consonants in words that contribute to intelligibility. This octave brings out articulations and transient details as well as making the mix brighter. Boosting too aggressively at this range will bring out sibilance.

9th Octave (5.12 kHz to 10.24 kHz). This octave emphasizes the brightness and high frequency details of the mix.

10th Octave (10.24 kHz to 20 kHz and up). Like the 1st octave, this octave is often more felt than heard. It is generally associated with a subjective airiness or open feeling. Too much level at this octave can bring out unwanted noise.

the optimal listening position. The LFE channel is mostly non-directional allowing for flexibility in speaker placement. The theatrical layout differs slightly in that the left and right screen channels are not angled and the surrounds are placed on the left and right walls rather than behind the listener. There are two basic approaches to 5.1 mixing: direct/ambient and inside the band. Many festivals (especially student festivals) screen films in stereo so it is important to clarify the mix format prior to submitting.

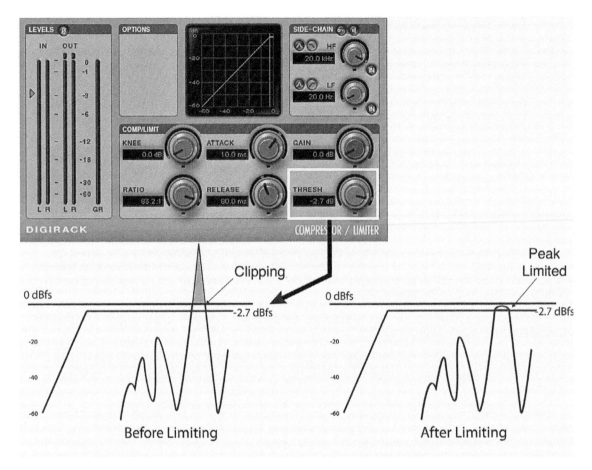

Figure 9.9 A Limiter is Designed to Prevent Occasional Peaks from Clipping

THE DIRECT/AMBIENT PERSPECTIVE

The direct/ambient perspective is the most widely accepted approach to mixing film in multi-channel. With this approach the discrete center channel carries the dialogue but can also be used to smooth the transition of sounds panned from left to right. As with stereo mixing, Foley elements linked to the dialogue are mixed in the center channel. The left and right channels carry underscore, hard effects, Walla, group ADR, and some BGs. BGs are also placed in the surrounds to envelop the audience in the environment. The surrounds can be used judiciously to enhance front to back movements such as a jet flyby. The LFE is used to carry the low frequency components of events like explosions, earthquakes, or the footsteps of a giant dinosaur. With

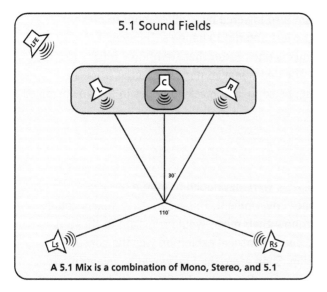

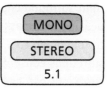

Figure 9.10 A 5.1 Mix is an Extension of a Stereo Mix, Having Mono Components As Well

the Direct/Ambient approach, audiences are listening in on a scene rather than being placed directly in the scene.

THE "INSIDE THE BAND" PERSPECTIVE

Mixing a film "inside the band" is an unconventional approach that stirs up much controversy with conventional re-recording mixers. With this approach, the surrounds are used more aggressively to deliver discrete sounds as well as BGs and underscore. The movement of off-screen objects can be exaggerated by panning dynamically around the room rather than moving from left to right in the screen channels. This approach to mixing is common in video games and to a lesser degree in films with 3D projection. The two main problems that arise when using this approach are *exit sign* effects and issues resulting from downmixing. The exit sign effect refers to discrete sounds playing in the surround channels that draw the audience away from the screen, thereby taking them out of the narrative experience. Downmixing (fold down) occurs when a mono or stereo playback system is used to playback a 5.1 soundtrack. The center channel and surrounds are redirected to the left and right channels to prevent the consumer from losing essential content. The center channel is lowered by -3 dB so that it sums in the phantom center at no additional level (unity gain). The left and right surround channels are also lowered by -3dB or more to prevent peaking and masking in the left and right channels. The need for a 5.1 mix to fold down to a stereo mix is one reason that traditional mixers use the surrounds conservatively. The additional content redirected from the surrounds can cause phase, peaking, and masking issues in the down-mixed version.

MASTERING FOR VARIOUS RELEASE FORMATS

In the mid 1980s, THX theaters were developed to match the mix environment to the playback environment. This meant that mixers could predict to a greater extent how their mixes would translate to theaters around the world. At that time, theatrical exhibition was the consumer's initial experience with a film. Soon after, the film would be released on various formats for home viewing. Gradually, the film would be premiered on a network. At each stage, the film would be modified to optimize playback for the specific release format. Today, the distribution model for media has expanded to include online delivery and personal devices. Content developers must consider these release formats and consumer monitoring options when developing mixes. Headphones or earbuds represent the single biggest shift in consumer listening habits. Consequently, it is now necessary to audition a mix on a good set of reference monitors, television speakers, and a set of ear buds, each time, noting differences that exist between playback and monitoring devices and adjusting the mix accordingly. With the exception of film and television, there are currently no mix standards for online delivery formats or personal devices. However, there are some guidelines that will contribute to a mix that effectively translates over multiple playback and monitoring devices:

- Mix at a level that approximates the listening habits of your target audience (reference level).
- A/B your mixes on the playback devices and monitors that consumers will be using and note how the mix is translating; a basic concept of mastering.
- Mix and master projects through monitoring plug-ins such as the Waves 360 Manager or the Sonnox mp3/AAC encoder.
- Add compression, especially on dialogue for non-theatrical release formats.

- Use fewer channels with greater transfer rates when quality is more important than the number of channels.
- Focus on the mid-range of the mix; this is the frequency range common to all playback devices and monitors.
- Codecs perform more accurately when processing files at higher sample rates and bit depths. Resolutions of 24 bit/48 kHz or higher are recommended although there is no advantage to up sampling prior to encoding.
- Since you cannot control the levels or type of monitoring used by a consumer, create a mix that conveys your vision for how the project should be experienced.

BOUNCING TO DISK OR TRACKS

Regardless of release format, the multitude of tracks present in a large mix session will ultimately be reduced to a mono, stereo, or multi-channel printmaster. The printmaster can be derived from bouncing the mix to disk or to tracks. When bouncing to disk, the outputs of the individual tracks are sent to the main output. During the bounce, no additional changes in leveling or panning can occur. When bouncing to tracks (internal layback), the outputs of individual tracks are hard bussed to one or more outputs, facilitating the printing of multiple printmasters in a single pass. When bouncing to tracks, additional fader and panner movements are possible. If the bounce is interrupted for any reason, the remaining portion of the mix can be punched in using the destructive record mode. In general, most mixers prefer bouncing to tracks.

ENCODING

DVD, BluRay, Internet, and personal devices all use codecs to address storage and transfer rate issues. These codecs utilize a variety of perceptual or redundancy encoding schemes to achieve data reduction and to set transfer rates. Audio resolution is affected to varying degrees with all lossy codecs. Content developers often pre-emphasize aspects of their mix to offset losses in frequency and dynamic range that result from encoding. It is important for the mixer to be able to monitor the mix through an encoder. In film, this is accomplished by monitoring the mix through hardware Dolby and DTS encoders. For mp3 and AAC encoding, Sonnox has created an auditioning plug-in that allows the mixer to compare settings of up to five different codecs in real-time (Figure 9.11). The user can toggle monitoring between the original input signal, the codec's output, or the difference signal (the audio that will be removed). This plug-in also provides estimations of how the resultant file size and transfer rates.

Encoding is an art unto itself, requiring a well-trained ear, a variety of monitoring options, and a bit of experimentation to optimize the mix for a multitude of monitoring systems and levels.

LAYBACK

Once the printmaster(s) is completed, it is then laid back or synched to picture. In file-based workflows, the audio is imported to picture-editing software such as Premier or Final Cut. For Internet and web based delivery, files undergo additional encoding. This is the point when all eyes and ears are focused on quality control. Once the layback is completed, the answer print is screened in a variety of playback environments to determine how well the mix is translating. Issues that show up during the layback sessions include:

- Sync issues caused by changes in frame rates, the use of video sync off-set for monitoring, or the soundtrack not being re-conformed to a recent picture edit.
- Distortion caused by the inappropriate monitoring levels, limitations in the playback device, or encoding errors.
- Missing audio, signals lost due to encoding, signals muted during bounce or improperly routed to print tracks.

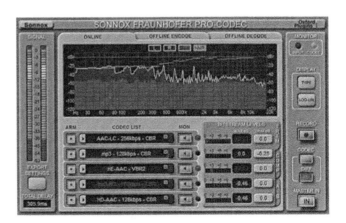

Figure 9.11 The Sonnox Fraunhofer Pro-Codec Encoder Allows the Context Developer to Audition the Mix with up to Five Different AAC or MP3 Settings

- Dull or lifeless mix, often caused by the encoding process or when monitoring at levels that are too low. Encoding issues can sometimes be mitigated by pre-emphasizing portions of the mix prior to encoding.

Once these issues are resolved and the printmaster is approved, the project is completed and ready for exhibition and distribution.

If you have the talent, and you keep trying . . . give it everything you've got on every job you get.

Thurl Ravenscroft

CHAPTER 10

CASE STUDIES

Many of the design principles discussed in this book can be heard on the great animation soundtracks of the past. With focused listening, we can reverse engineer these soundtracks and effectively reveal the many creative ideas contained within. These design principles can then become the foundation for designing soundtracks on future films. The timings provided in the following case studies are approximations based on the playback timings displayed on a standard DVD player. Take time to LISTEN to these films, noting the special contributions made by these creative composers and sound designers. Learn to read the unwritten books.

Learn to read the unwritten books.

Ancient Chinese Proverb

101 DALMATIONS, DISNEY (1961) SOUND: ROBERT COOK, SCORE: GEORGE BRUNS

00:00   This title sequence is an exemplary study in hits and isomorphism.

ALADDIN, DISNEY (1992) SOUND: MARK MANGINI, SCORE: ALEN MENKEN & TIM RICE

08:58   A car skid and bowling pin crash are used to exaggerate movements in this foot chase.

20:07   Jafar's evil laugh post-laps to next scene.

36:13   An isomorphic cue is created to emphasize the handshake between the Genie and the Magic Carpet.

42:39   The parrot swooping movement is exaggerated by layering it (sweetening) with the sound of a dive-bomber.

53:20   The dialogue levels and reverb shift with the picture cut to establish Jasmine's proximity to her suitors.

1:16:28   The sound of Sebastian's jaw dropping is exaggerated with window blinds.

1:18:40   Jafar's voice morphs into a snake.

ALICE IN WONDERLAND (1951) SOUND: C.O. SLYFIELD, SCORE: OLIVER WALLACE

08:56   The underscore hits with each line of dialogue. "I'm Locked" (door knob) "Oh no" (Alice).

ALPHA AND OMEGA (2010) SOUND: PAULA FAIRFIELD, SCORE: CHRIS BACON

17:35   Disco era music creates a romantic backdrop for Humphrey's misdirection. The cue ends with a phonograph needle rip as Humphrey realizes he is hugging one of his friends rather than Kate (his love interest).

23:00   Heavy reverb is added to Kate's dialogue representing her subject state, induced by a tranquilizer gun.

57:15   Tonal wolf howls seamlessly integrated into the score.

1:05:25   Diegetic sound fades during this sequence to allow the audience to focus on the thoughts of the principal characters.

ANASTASIA (1997) SOUND: RICHARD ANDERSON, SCORE: DAVID NEWMAN

04:01   The crash of a chandelier post-laps into next scene (ring-out).

11:12   Slavic underscore hits with each line of dialogue spoken by Comrade Phlegmenkoff: "and be grateful too."

12:28   The speaking voice of Meg Ryan transitions to the singing voice of Liz Calloway in the song "Journey to the Past." This rendition is orchestrated in a musical style rather than in a pop style to create a timeless feeling.

17:55   Reverb and volume are added to the underscore to support the flashback and to initiate the transition from underscore to song.

29:05   Rasputin's performance of "In the Dark of the Night" is performed in a recitative style.

38:17   The sound of the train falling is treated with Doppler.

50:09   Various BGs are used to toggle back and forth from Anastasia's dream state and the reality of her present danger.

1:12:56   The thunder post-laps via a ring-out.

THE ANT BULLY (2006) SOUND: MARK MENZA, SCORE: JOHN DEBNEY

19:07   The cue is an extended isomorphism. Zach's screams are treated with Doppler as he hurls downward into the ant bed.

35:00   The sound of the firecracker fuse plays loudly, representing Zach's shrunken perspective. The explosion that follows plays softly, reinforcing the perspective created by the camera shift.

1:09:00   A Viennese waltz creates an anempathetic feel as the exterminator sprays the ants with his lethal concoction.

ANTZ (1998) SOUND: RICHARD ANDERSON, SCORE: STEVE JABLONSKY

17:18   The source music, "Almost like being in love," contains narrative lyrics and sets up the misdirection that will follow. The factory horn is pitched to the key of the song and is a transitional device, moving from source to underscore. The instrumentation thins out and the tempo slows down to support the time lapse.

22:19   The song provides narrative lyrics "The Ants go Marching."

56:21   This montage sequence is scored with an updated cover of the pop single "I Can See Clearly Now."

1:10:25   Dialogue is used to bridge a cut as Z hands off the line to Princess Bala at the picture edit.

THE ARISTOCATS (1970) SOUND: ROBERT COOK, SCORE: GEORGE BRUNS

00:00   The title sequence music is an establishing element for the French setting. The second verse is sung in French without subtitles.

05:26   The source music emitting from the gramophone establishes the time period while sonically transitioning the audience through various rooms in the house.

ATLANTIS: THE LOST EMPIRE (2001) SOUND: DANE DAVIS, SCORE: JAMES NEWTON HOWARD

00:43   Atlantean dialogue is spoken and translated via subtitles.

02:33   The sound of a manual typewriter accompanies screen text which indicates location and date. Milo's off-screen dialogue pre-pals as the camera moves from exterior to interior, revealing the misdirection that is his audience.

31:09   The music cue hits with each of Audrey's playful punches.

38:24   The picture goes to black just before the vehicles crash. The off-screen sound completes the action and softens the perception of the scene's violence.

40:55   Milo's dialogue is treated with echo to show the vastness of the environment.

44:20   Atlantean dialogue is spoken with subtitles. The transition to spoken English occurs in response to Commander Rourke's introductory remarks.

52:17   The sound of stilts moving in water pre-pals in sync with a visual wipe.

1:00:14   Off-screen sound completes the action of Rourke punching King Nedakh, which allows the violence to be implicit.

1:03:01   Princess Kida's voice is digitally treated as she reverts to her Atlantean language.

BEE MOVIE (2007) SOUND: WILL FILES/MICHAEL SILVERS, SCORE: RUPERT GREGSON-WILLIAMS

06:30   SFX are muted during the freeze frames, yet the underscore plays through the shot.

16:39   The underscore slows down as the bees de-accelerate and land on the tennis court. The Theremin is used to create an uneasy feel for the backgrounds. The SFX are exaggerated in level and low frequency content to establish the Bee's perspective.

19:03   The underscore suddenly stops as the mother yells "freeze."

30:04   The dialogue gets muffled as Barry submerges in the pool of honey. This treatment is part of the transition to the montage sequence, scored with the song "Sugar Sugar." The emotional character of the music and lyrics sets up the ensuing misdirection.

40:30   The dialogue pre-lap implies narration but is soon revealed as diegetic.

44:30   The venetian score implies that Barry is floating on a Gondola rather than a sugar cube. A sonic analogy.

1:10:50   Cockpit voices are futzed when off-screen and play in full resolution when on-screen.

BOLT (2008) SOUND: FRANK EULER, SCORE: JOHN POWELL

09:12   The silence before the explosion helps exaggerate the intensity of the explosion.

11:25   This scene features a postproduction room where the source audio is futzed to imply raw footage and production audio. The boom pool adds a nice visual touch.

1:00:05   The caged dogs in the kennel speak the word ball in English. As the camera shifts to the perspective of a human kennel worker, the word ball morphs into real dogs barking.

1:16:18   Rhino (the hamster) dialogue is presented in English until the POV shifts to the actor who only hears hamster squeaks.

BROTHER BEAR (2003) SOUND: RICHARD ANDERSON, SCORE: PHIL COLLINS/MARK MANCINA

49:50   This shot features a narrative play on echoes as the rams unwittingly address themselves.

1:01:02   Slavic music and Russian dialogue establishes the ethnicity of the bear.

A BUG'S LIFE (1998) SOUND: TIM HOLLAND/ GARY RYDSTROM, SCORE: RANDY NEWMAN

0:00   The opening scene begins with BGs rather than music.

19:20   The underscore for Flick in flight is suddenly interrupted when he hits the rock (misdirection).

20:04   The initial dialogue treatment for the bug fight sets up a misdirection as it is soon revealed to be a stage production.

27:28   The isomorphic scratching of the violin dramatically covers the sound of an inebriated bug scratching his legs.

29:53   Slim's (Walking Stick) dialogue "Swish swish, clang clang" is making fun of clichéd sound design.

35:48   This cue is an extended pre-lap that functions like underscore to source.

38:14   The megaphone is futzed with added feedback loop for realism.

42:40   An accelerated whoosh plays in sync with camera zoom.

44:50   The off-screen applause transitions to on-screen, finally post-lapping to an interior shot with Francis (Ladybug) recuperating.

48:25   A single line of dialogue is broken up and delivered by multiple characters, bridging a series of visual cuts.

52:49   The underscore is later revealed as source as the camera moves from exterior to interior. The song "La Cucaracha" establishes the proximity of grasshoppers from the ant colony.

1:20:44   A loud beetle roar is followed by the sound of an injured dog, implying a role reversal.

1:21:17   Raindrops are sweetened with the sounds of jet engines and missiles to represent the magnitude of rain from a bug's perspective.

CARS (2006) SOUND: TOM MYERS/MICHAEL SILVERS, SCORE: RANDY NEWMAN

12:00   Reverb is gradually added to the dialogue as the narrative transitions from reality to fantasy.

18:05   A cover version of "Life is a Highway" provides narrative lyrics for the traveling sequence. The ringing of a phone masks the transition of the cue from underscore to source.

40:19   A dialogue ring-out is used as a transitional device.

1:42:40   The diegetic sounds of the raceway fade out and the underscore fades up as the scene becomes subjective.

CHICKEN LITTLE (2005) SOUND: ROBERT SEPHTON, SCORE: JOHN DEBNEY

10:12   The sound of a bull whip creates an exaggerated feel for the coach whipping out a dodge ball.

10:30   The donkey kicks are exaggerated with machine gun fire.

15:30   Heavily reverberant bat cracks and crowd cheers support the flashback as the backstory is presented.

28:50   Excessively loud singing triggers car alarms, providing an off-screen commentary on the quality of Chicken Little's voice.

58:00   The song "It's the End of the World" provides narrative lyrics for the Alien invasion. Subtitles are provided for the Inter-galactic dialogue.

1:11:3   The whip cracking sound is used to exaggerate the captain's neck movements, creating an over-the-top feel for the scene.

CHICKEN RUN (2000) SOUND: JAMES MATHER/ GRAHAM HEADICAR, SCORE: HENRY GREGSON-WILLIAMS/ JOHN POWELL

11:55	Accordions and wedding bells are added to underscore as sweeteners to reinforce the narrative implications.
12:40	"Ave Maria" is futzed as the camera moves from the farmhouse exterior to the interior. This choice of music creates anempathetic feel for the scene.
15:15	The underscore builds toward a misdirection.
28:20	The underscore temporarily transitions to pentatonic scale to play on the karate portion of their training.
47:00	The Group ADR fades as the romantic jazz underscore fades up to push the subjectivity and emotion of the scene.
102:05	The Group ADR fades as the cue is brought out to reinforce the subjective moment.
1:06:18	Futzed source music pre-pals to the next scene. The narrative lyrics support Rocky's willful abandoning of the chicken coup and love interest.

CINDERELLA (1950) SOUND: ROBERT COOK, SCORE: DAVID, HOFFMAN, AND LIVINGSTON

9:50	A Harp gliss plays isomorphically in sync with the opening of the curtains.
14:00	Underscored sneak steps are used for on and off-screen movements.
24:15	Reverb is added to the dialogue for contrast as the helmet is closed.
25:58	Isomorphic figures support the camera moves. The reverb shifts as the characters move from room to room.

CORPSE BRIDE (2005) SOUND: EDDY JOSEPH,
SCORE: DANNY ELFMAN

19:44   The lyrics to the song "Die Die" provides the back-story for the bride. The instrumentation (marimbas and xylophones) is consistent with the skeleton characters. This cue post-laps with an extended ring-out.

CURIOUS GEORGE (2006) SOUND: DARREN KING/
GREGORY KING, SCORE: HIETOR PEREIRA

27:00   The score and the elevator bell progressively pitch up as the elevator ascends.

DINOSAUR (2000) SOUND: FRANK EULNER,
SCORE: JAMES NEWTON HOWARD

04:20   The soundtrack features nearly three minutes of varied BGs as the egg moves through many environments.

10:45   The angry growls, monkey screams, and intense underscore set up the misdirection.

18:27   The soundtrack gets silent just prior to the meteor hitting the earth, providing dynamic contrast.

20:06   BGs are treated with bandwidth filtering to support the shift from the surface to the submerged shot.

49:49   The off-screen dripping sounds develop the characteristics of the cave.

56:57   In this clip is heard an extended post-lap of a scream using the ring out technique.

1:03:33   Hard effects and BGs start from one side of the mountain and transition to the other.

DESPICABLE ME (2010) SOUND: CHRISTOPHER SCARABOSIO, SCORE: HEITOR PEREIRA/ PHARRELL WILLIAMS

01:24	Epic underscore sets up the misdirection for Shepherd getting hit by a bus.
15:42	Song "The Girl from Ipanema" pre-laps and later post-laps with a substantial reverb ring out.
28:01	Vari-speed is applied to the underscore.
43:00	Gru counts to three, just prior to the third number, we cut to the dance studio with the dance teacher saying "three."
55:49	Whoosh follows camera for both zoom in and out.

EVERYONE'S HERO (2006) SOUND: SEAN GARNHART, SCORE: JOHN DEBNEY

02:18	Underscore builds toward misdirection.
04:20	Futzed newsreel with added pitch warping to suggest a faltering projector. Dialogue implies narration but is soon revealed to be diegetic.
06:30	The score builds to the visual wipe (film burning). The film sprocket sounds morph to the sewing machine as a transitional device (form edit).
07:00	Yankee's thoughts are treated with reverb and echo to support the subjective moment.
08:20	The sound of a pin ball hitting bumpers is used to exaggerate the sound of the baseball bouncing off surfaces in the bedroom.
57:55	The cue transitions from source to underscore, introducing a modern musical style in a period film.

FINDING NEMO (2003) SOUND: GARY RYDSTROM, SCORE: THOMAS NEWMAN

07:20   The sound of a tire's screeching represents the school of fish coming to a sudden halt.

13:40   Reverb and level are used to shift the dialogue from on-screen to off-screen. This treatment promotes the ever-increasing distance between Marlin and Nemo, a concept that will become the center of the conflict.

24:56   There is a deliberate pause in the soundtrack just before the explosions to create contrast. Then, when the picture cuts to the surface, a lone bubble comically reduces the off-screen action to little more than flatulence.

26:50   The rapid movement of the fish tail is exaggerated using castanets. Jacque's ethnicity is established with French accordion music.

31:42   The underscore descends and then ascends isomorphically with Marlin's movements.

56:00   Lines of dialogue cross fades from character to character as a transitional device. This sequence ends with a flock of seagulls (voiced by humans) saying "Mine Mine" to reinforce on their greedy nature (Group ADR).

1:05:30 Dory communicates using whale speak.

1:15:36 This music cue is a cultural referent from the film "*Psycho*." The ensuing dialogue post-laps via a ring out.

1:25:10 Dialogue lines are time compressed to reinforce the flashback.

FLUSHED AWAY (2006) SOUND: RICHARD ANDERSON, SCORE: HARRY GREGSON-WILLIAMS

10:45   This isomorphic cue builds to promote the misdirection.

29:17   Rita's individual words are emphasized with orchestral hits.

47:06   The frog tongues are exaggerated with the sounds of metal swords.

GNOMEO AND JULIET (2011) SOUND: GLENN FREEMANTLE, SCORE: JAMES NEWTON HOWARD/ ELTON JOHN

12:45   Nanette the frog says "you look hot" in Japanese translated in subtitles. Soon after, she says another line in Japanese, this time the subtitles are left out because the action implies the meaning.

22:36   Nanette's laugh is sweetened with water bubbles.

23: 38   Nanette's dialogue pans from center to hard right as she prances off-screen.

31:15   Mock-up commercial on Terfirminator using heavy metal music and futzed dialogue, ending with a TC/E disclaimer.

42:39   A parody of Elton John's "This Song" is modified to include lyrics about pesticide and miracle grow. This parody is used to unfavorably characterize Juliet's un-wanted suitor.

1:01:25   Gnome inadvertently plays "Bennie and the Jets" as he walks on the computer keyboard and finger pad.

HERCULES (1997) SOUND: TIM HOLLAND, SCORE: ALAN MENKEN

00:15   Charlton Heston's opening narration is interrupted by the gospel chorus to provide a modern version of the backstory.

04:58   The underscore builds, followed by a whoosh that follows the camera movement.

06:55   Pain's footsteps are literal until he falls down the stairs. These movements are playfully covered to de-emphasize the violence.

14:04   An off-screen jet pass-by is used to introduce the wooden cart. This is followed by an off-screen descending whistle which sets up the on-screen donkey landing.

29:38   A glockenspiel plays the circular wipe (isomorphism) represented visually by leaves.

44:35   Hades' dialogue post-laps with a ring out on the phrase "Lets get ready to rumble."

1:00:04   The underscore builds toward the kiss which is interrupted by the helicopter sound substituted for horse wings.

HOME ON THE RANGE (2004) SOUND: TIM CHAU, SCORE: ALAN MENKEN

14:45   The dialogue fades following the camera zoom out.

15:00   This dream sequence ends in a misdirection. The dialogue is treated with reverb and is time scaled to transition out of the dream.

47:02   Underscore is isomorphic, following the camera movements.

51:05   Reverb effectively defines both interior and exterior.

HOODWINKED! (2005) SOUND: TOM MYERS, SCORE: JOHN PAINTER/KRISTIN WILKINSON

00:12   35 mm camera sound provides the foundation for the title sequence.

04:48   Underscore pre-laps for a back-story sequence and post-laps with a ring out transitioning to present time.

08:10   The voices in this phone split are not treated for perspective since both characters are on camera.

08:55   The sound of an off-screen car crash is used to imply the action, thereby softening its impact.

19:06   An example of reverse as the lumberjack flies back through the window.

20:35   Cultural referent for the live action film "Fletch."

24:28   Futzed signal with radio interference added to reinforce the on-screen parabolic microphone.

25:08   Red Riding Hood's screams are briefly interrupted for each camera flash yet the music plays through the scene. The audio shifts in perspective for each camera angle.

40:42   Reverb is progressively added to the dialogue, transitioning to the montage sequence.

1:01:26 The sound for the slow motion shot is treated with echo to play the subjectivity of the shot.

HOW TO TRAIN YOUR DRAGON (2010) SOUND: RANDY THOM/JONATHAN NULL, SCORE: JOHN POWELL

50:55 Hiccup's dialogue line bridges the edit between the arena and the secret lair of the dragon.

1:00:30 Reverb is added to Stoick's address to support perspective shifts to the arena where Hiccup prepares to battle the dragon.

THE HUNCHBACK OF NOTRE DAME (1996) SOUND: LON BENDER, SCORE: ALAN MENKEN

00:00 Church bells and Gregorian chant serve as establishing elements in title sequence.

07:45 The cue builds as Hugo prepares to spit on the crowd below.

18:15 Isomorphism for the twitch of the guard's mustache.

19:24 The backgrounds allow the audience to hear the previous captain being whipped off-screen, keeping the violence implicit.

20:10 The music hits with each word spoken by Frollo.

42:50 This is an extended isomorphism which is skillfully varied.

1:00:42 Quasimodo's interior thoughts and feelings are presented in non-sync song, allowing him to make comment without interfering with the action.

1:15:55 Machine gun sounds are substituted for stones to exaggerate the visuals.

1:16:42 A WW II airplane by is used to cover the soldier flying through the air.

1:16:48 Cultural reference of the Witch in *The Wizard of Oz* commanding the flying monkeys.

ICE AGE (2002) SOUND: SEAN GARNHART, SCORE: DAVID NEWMAN

00:25   The opening sequence is an extended feature of realistic BGs.

30:12   In this slow motion sequence, the music is not treated but the dialogue and FX are processed and pitched down.

31:22   Birds scream post-laps and a music cue pre-laps during this creative visual wipe.

49:48   Reverb is added to the hard effects to support the back-story provided visually through cave drawings.

ICE AGE: THE MELTDOWN (2006) SOUND: DOUGLAS MURRAY, SCORE: WILL EDWARDS/ JOHN POWELL

08:41   Cue hits with each word in the dialogue "still have ice."

15:06   Reverb is added to dialogue as the character sticks his head into the hole.

38:40   Whooshes are used as transitional sound for flashback.

59:50   The sound is muffled to play the subjectivity of the moment.

THE INCREDIBLES (2004) SOUND: MICHAEL SILVERS, SCORE: MICHAEL GIACCHINO

0:00   Opening sequence music switches from underscore to source to underscore.

5:20   Isomorphic cue to represent Elastigirl vaulting across rooftops.

6:48   French music is used to develop the Bomb Voyage character.

10:11   Dialogue is futzed to imply a television interview.

11:34   The BGs establish the monotonous environment of an office cubicle.

16:30   Bob's rickety car is designed to show how "normal" he has become.

18:46   The dialogue is treated to shift perspective from kitchen to bedroom.

24:20   Bob hums along with the theme song underscore, blurring the lines between source and underscore.

26:54   Multiple futzed signals playing at the same time.

31:45   Both Mirage and Helen's off-screen dialogue are futzed.

41:24   The montage sequence begins with a bongo drum roll pre-lap.

43:00   Futzing for Edna's security gate speaker, cars pan off-camera as well.

53:00   The music cue hits when Mr. Incredible sees a dead super.

1:20:20 Dash's footsteps get treated with reverb as he moves through environments.

1:23:53 Dialogue pans off-center in sync with character movements.

IRON GIANT (1999) SOUND: DENNIS LEONARD, SCORE: MICHAEL KAMEN

06:11   The phone ring pre-laps and the off-screen voices of the phone split are futzed.

21:02   The dialogue of the Giant is digitally treated.

56:55   This cue is a tick tock, marking time and influencing the pacing.

JIMMY NEUTRON: BOY GENIUS (2001) SOUND: CHRISTOPHER WELCH, SCORE: JOHN DEBNEY/ BRIAN CAUSEY

10:05   The teacher has a caw-like quality added to her voice, caricaturing her beak-like nose.

13:32   A ring-out is added at the end of the teacher's scream.

17:02   Jimmy's off-screen fall is treated with a descending whistle and reverb for added perspective.

17:57	Tween cover of "He Blinded Me With Science" updates the tune and shifts the gender focus.
20:20	Futzed game show music with vari-speed effect.
1:04:25	Source music "The Chicken Dance" heard from a distance to establish proximity.

THE JUNGLE BOOK (1967) SOUND: ROBERT COOK, SCORE: GEORGE BRUNS

9:52	Kaa's voice has deliberate sibilance to caricature the snake hiss.
12:12	An accordion is used to cover the snake tail expanding and contracting (isomorphism). The sound of a rusty hinge is added to indicate that Kaa's tail is broken.
23:55	The score accelerates as Mowgli's pace picks up.
31:51	Delay is used to show the disorientation of Bagheera.
39:16	The score cadences in a manner that sounds more like a commercial break than a visual transition for a film.

LADY AND THE TRAMP (1955) SOUND: ROBERT COOK, SCORE: OLIVER WALLACE

11:06	Jock the Scottish Terrier is voiced with a Scottish accent.
13:40	Trusty the Hound is voiced with southern accent.
17:40	Bull the English Bulldog is voiced with a classic English accent.
22:22	A bassoon is used to create the sneak steps for the dogs.
23:00	Isomorphic cue is used to exaggerate head turns.
31:26	Oriental music for Siamese cats.
53:05	Schultzie the Dachshund is voiced with a German accent.
54:00	Boris the Afghan is voiced with a Russian accent.
55.35	Pedro the Mexican Chihuahua is voiced with a Mexican accent.

THE LION KING (1994) SOUND: RICHARD ANDERSON/MARK MANGINI, SCORE: HANS ZIMMER

07:06	Varied BGs are used to define space and show time lapse.
26:07	Reverberant off-screen dialogue pre-laps.
32:55	Simba's growls are initially dry then treated to echo.
37:45	The echo helps reinforce Simba's isolation and helplessness.
50:34	The vocal pre-lap is treated with reverb, transitioning from off-screen to on-screen.
54:47	Pumbaa the warthog's scream is sweetened with elephant trumpet.
107:04	Reverb is applied to Mufasa's voice to contrast him from his living son.
117:23	Bowling pins exaggerate Pumbaa's charge through the crowd of hyenas.
119:59	Reverb and pitching supports the slow motion (subjective) sequence.

THE LITTLE MERMAID (1989) SOUND: LOUIS EDEMANN/ RICHARD FRANKLIN, SCORE: ALAN MENKEN

25:25	Empty metal can drop sound is used to cover Sebastian's jaw dropping.
32:41	Foley crab footsteps are blended with musical sneak steps.
45:45	Piccolo isomorphism for Ariel's wiggling her newly acquired feet.
50:38	A door hinge and slam used to cover Sebastian passing out.
58:30	Off-screen dialogue transitions to on-screen, saving on time-consuming lip animation. The BGs in this sequence are prominent as well.
106:43	Boxing ring fight bell is used to exaggerate Scuttle's impact against the boat.
1:08:39	Dive-bombers used to cover birds attacking the boat.

MADAGASCAR (2005) SOUND: RICHARD ANDERSON, SCORE: HANS ZIMMER

9:31   Pointalistic "Happy Birthday" followed by a whoosh that is motivated by a camera move.

15:20   Alex makes a humorous reference to ambience tracks. A powering-down sound is used to transition to urban ambience.

23:32   Subjective treatment for Alex getting drugged.

30:54   Dialogue post-lap accomplished with ring out.

32:40   Cultural referent of *Hawaii 5.0* with vari-speed effect, followed by quote from *Chariots of Fire*.

55:00   Parody on *American Beauty*, reverb ring-out is outpoint.

MEET THE ROBINSONS (2007) SOUND: TODD TOON, SCORE: DANNY ELFMAN

18:35   Bowler Hat Guy laughing with extended post-lap.

44:14   Off-screen voice-over futzed.

51:50   Multiple whooshes follow the camera movements.

104:25 Dialogue playing across the time lapse. Futzed radio supports time lapse.

108:12 Harp isomorphism for descending then ascending visuals.

110:00 The sound on the archive video is futzed to sonically imply that the footage is aged.

MEGAMIND (2010) SOUND: ERIK AADAHL, SCORE: HANS ZIMMER/LORNE BALFE

01:53   Impacts are pitched to the score.

14:18   This form edit morphs a painful scream into an adoring crowd.

29:30   Echo

45:42   A whoosh follows the camera move.

53:30   The ring of the wine glasses are pitched in the resolution of the underscore.

1:02:43   Score hits with each floor crash.

MONSTER HOUSE (2006) SOUND: RANDY THOM/ DENNIS LEONARD, SCORE: DOUGLAS PIPES

14:36   Dream sequence misdirection.

25:40   Pitch shifted doorbell foreshadows what is to come.

MONSTERS VS. ALIENS (2009) SOUND: ERIK AAHAHL/ ETHAN VAN DER RYN, SCORE: HENRY JACKMAN

00:05   Title sequence has a vari-speed effect and a vinyl rip added to play the 35 mm print burning.

02:22   Creepy breathing and light flashes establish the misdirection revealed when Susan's friends wake her on her wedding day.

23:33   Screams are post-lapped with a ring-out.

52:52   Derek's (weatherman) dialogue transitions from futzed (looking through the camera) to full frequency when he is off-camera.

MULAN (1998) SOUND: LON BENDER, SCORE: JERRY GOLDSMITH

20:38   Ancestors' voices are treated with lots of reverb to contrast them from the living. The voice of the Chinese dragon is played by an African-American comedian (Eddie Murphy) yet there is no disconnect.

26:50   The absence of sound during the visual black makes the impending violence even more implicit.

46:02   A typewriter covers the sound of ChaCha (the cricket) writing a letter in Chinese script as he hops on the page.

59:38   Subjective moment as Ping looses consciousness. Dialogue is processed with reverb to create the transition.

THE NIGHTMARE BEFORE CHRISTMAS (1993) SOUND: RICHARD ANDERSON, SCORE: DANNY ELFMAN

06:17   Recitative style of story delivery.

11:24   Doorbell sweetener of girl screaming.

38:02   Minor version of "Jingle Bells" plays the disconnect with the season.

50:38   Minor version of "Here comes Santa Claus", plays the distorted narrative.

108:18   News announcer's voice transitions from full frequency to futzed as the shot transitions to television.

OVER THE HEDGE (2006) SOUND: RICHARD ANDERSON, SCORE: RUPERT GREGSON-WILLIAMS

24:20   Dream sequence ends in misdirection.

34:11   The off-screen sound of screeching tires completes the off-screen crash, making the action more implicit and less violent.

34:55   The POV shifts as the opossum talks in English for the audience and squeaks when viewed from the human characters perspective.

110:59   The slow motion sequence is treated by removing all diegetic sound, leaving only underscore.

POCAHONTAS (1995) SOUND: LON BENDER/LARRY KEMP, SCORE: ALAN MENKEN

08:43   The above and below surface environments have changes in EQ and reverb to provide contrast.

30:15   Pocahontas's speech transitions from Native Indian to English.

THE POLAR EXPRESS (2004) SOUND: DENNIS LEONARD, SCORE: ALAN SILVERSTRI

05:00   The sound of the clock transitions from the present reality to the subjectivity that is the extended dream sequence.

14:30	A harp gliss covers the camera move (isomorphism).
15:35	The sound of the train engine morphs into a percussive element of the score.
110:48	The BGs and Walla fade and the source music is treated with vari-speed.
128:15	The clock is used as a transitional device, moving out of the dream sequence.

THE PRINCE OF EGYPT (1998) SOUND: WYLIE STATEMAN, SCORE: HANS ZIMMER/STEPHEN SCHWARTZ

21:35	The song is the narrative element that links Moses to his past. The song is sung in his thoughts, perhaps to conceal his understanding from the Egyptians.
39:01	The song "Through Heaven's Eyes" is presented as a montage but ends with source music.
54:38	This recitative style of song delivery is common for the villains in animated musicals.

THE PRINCESS AND THE FROG (2009) SOUND: ODIN BENITEZ, SCORE: RANDY NEWMAN

06:30	BGs pre-lap to support the time lapse.
08:52	SFX are integrated rhythmically with the song.
41:06	The wave sound whooshes as a transitional device from the swamp to the Antebellum home.
1:12:58	The Riverboat horn pre-laps.

PUSS IN BOOTS (2011) SOUND: RICHARD KING, SCORE: HENRY JACKSON

12:05	SFX morph into score in the dance fight sequence.
28:10	The SFX and dialogue in this subjective moment are pitched and rhythmically slowed down.

RANGO (2011) SOUND: ADDISON TEAGUE, SCORE: HANS ZIMMER

4:54   *Ave Maria* underscores the slow motion shot that ends in the terrarium crashing through the car window. The underscore is abruptly interrupted to transition back to reality.

5:52   Exaggerated sounds as Rango is exposed to the intense heat. The sound of the water drop exiting the glass implies a dry spigot. The water sizzles as it hits his tongue for an exaggerated effect.

14:04   The lizards line "you son of a" . . . (interrupt) . . . Hawk squeak, infers the profanity rather than being overt.

1:05:22   Wagner's "Ride of the Valkyries" is customized with banjo, jew's harp, and harmonica to give it a western feel.

RATATOUILLE (2007) SOUND: RANDY THOM, SCORE: MICHAEL GIACCHINO

02:00   Narration seamlessly transitions to and from the principal dialogue using level and no reverb.

04:19   The television is futzed but the underscore is not.

08:50   Gusteau's cooking show is futzed.

10:17   The dialogue changes from English to rat squeaks as the POV switches between the rats and the gun-wielding old lady. This treatment suggests a design rule that rats are not to talk to humans.

16:08   Additional reverb reinforces the sonic movement as Gusteau is sucked into the bottle. "Food always comes . . ."

21:04   Flutter trumpets stay on same note while strings play a descending line as Remy falls from the ceiling into the kitchen (isomorphism).

25:08   When we are listening to the dialogue through Remy's ears, reverb is added.

39:18   Off-screen crash is heard rather than seen to de-emphasize the action.

57:01 The dialogue pre-lap is extended, as the father says "My son has returned . . ."

1:13:10 The underscore hits with each of Remy's words.

1:23:30 Heartbeats morph to footsteps and a door knock as we transition out of the dream sequence.

1:36:25 Transitional whooshes that follow the camera move, followed by exaggerated FX for slow motion pen dropping to floor.

1:41:13 Voice over to diegetic dialogue as Remy is revealed as the storyteller.

RIO (2011) SOUND: RANDY THOM/GWENDOLYN WHITTLE, SCORE: JOHN POWELL

00:35 Title sequence begins with ambience that morphs into a Samba. Each type of bird contributes to the musical layers.

12:15 The sound of the airplane pre-pals as Linda and Blu fly to Rio.

56:52 Boxing ring bell morphs into a trolley bell (form edit).

65:00 The SFX and dialogue in this subjective scene are pitched down and rhythmically slowed down, yet the underscore remains unaffected.

72:30 1980s pop ballad is used to creates a romantic mood which gets interrupted (misdirection) as Blu and Jewel's beaks collide.

82:25 Nigel's ultimate doom is completed with off-screen sound.

THE ROAD TO EL DORADO (2000) SOUND: GREGORY KING, SCORE: JOHN POWELL/HANS ZIMMER

03:10 Car tire skids are used to exaggerate the arm extension. A door opening is used for hand movements over the eyes.

44.00 The score builds toward misdirection, ending in a vinyl rip.

ROBIN HOOD (1973) SOUND: JIMMY MCDONALD, SCORE: GEORGE BRUNS

06:43   Sir Hiss's voice has a deliberate sibilance.

45:20   The rock underscore takes you out of the period.

ROBOTS (2005) SOUND: SEAN GARNHART, SCORE: JOHN POWELL

0:00   The ticking clock morphs into the underscore. The clock is a metaphor for what makes a robot tick.

5:28   Television source music is futzed.

8:07   Off-key underscore "Pomp and Circumstance" establishes the narrative that he is graduating. The time lapse is designed with 35 mm snapshots sounds.

10:10   A vari-speed effect is used to reinforce the failure of the dishwasher.

18:30   The tempo of the cue follows closely with the visual pacing.

20:05   The underscore sets up the misdirection.

23:55   This isomorphic cue ends with three hits.

31:55   The SFX are pitched up even as the robot falls.

37:30   Aunt Fanny's large posterior is exaggerated using the beeping sound of a truck backing up.

40:30   The impact of the flatulence sounds are exaggerated with car alarms.

52:34   "Singing in the Oil" is an homage to "Singing in the Rain," this rendition sets up a misdirection.

100:58   Extended post-lap as Fender screams for help.

119:45   Bigweld asks the microphone to stop echoing.

SHARK TALE (2004) SOUND: RICHARD ANDERSON, SCORE: HANS ZIMMER

00:45	"Jaws" theme quoted (cultural referent) to set up a misdirection.
03:51	Title music gets interrupted with quiet Sushi Bar music for comic effect.
11:00	Voice pitches up when blowfish expands.
25:00	Dialogue is pitched down for slow motion sequence.
35:28	Each time the words "Shark Slayer" are said, a cue begins.
45:05	Lenny realizes that there is an echo and refers directly to it.
1:14:58	Subjective treatment for slow motion shot.

SHREK (2001) SOUND: LON BENDER/WYLIE STATEMAN, SCORE: HARRY GREGSON-WILLIAMS/JOHN POWELL

00:00	The opening music establishes a fairy tale mood that sets up a misdirection.
14:00	Shrek's yell is treated with an audible delay.
20:38	The panning for this character movement is very literal.
21:20	The source music is typical lounge music in a Latin style, a comedic choice for a film set in the mythical time period.
48:45	The dialogue for the magic mirror is treated with vari-speed and reverse effects.
52:55	The cue suspends harmonically as the princess prepares to kick the two men.

SHREK 2 (2004) SOUND: DENNIS LEONARD, SCORE: HARRY GREGSON-WILLIAMS

02:34	35 mm projection sound is added to reinforce the home footage look.
15:00	The cue pre-laps.
103:33	The magic wand sounds transitioning to fireworks (form edit).

SHREK III (2007) SOUND: RICHARD ANDERSON/
THOMAS JONES, SCORE: HARRY GREGSON-WILLIAMS

00:22   The opening music sets up the misdirection as the horse is soon revealed as a prop. The soundtrack is gradually futzed as camera zooms out.

08:07   Underscore ends abruptly as the window shade is closed, showing his unwillingness to show feeling toward the cat.

09:30   The music supports the misdirection of the King's death.

19:21   The ship's horn masks Fiona's proclamation that Shrek is a dad.

21:07   The sound supports a double dream sequence.

36:41   Whooshes are used for each transition as the gingerbread man's life passes before his eyes.

52:15   Underscore to source cue as the piano is revealed and Donkey says "lookout, they have a piano."

THE SIMPSONS (2007) SOUND: GWENDOLYN YATES
WHITTLE, SCORE: HANS ZIMMER

00:33   Parody on *Also Sprach Zarathustra* morphing into the Simpsons' theme.

110:18   Misdirection

116:28   Isomorphic cue follows camera move.

SINBAD: LEGEND OF THE SEVEN SEAS (2003)
SOUND: CHARLES CAMPBELL/RICHARD FRANKLIN,
SCORE: HARRY GREGSON-WILLIAMS

108:30   Cue builds toward a misdirection.

SURF'S UP (2007) SOUND: STEVEN TICKNOR,
SCORE: MYCHAEL DANNA

07:42   The dialogue pre-laps and is scored with futzed Hawaiian music playing on the radio. The boom pole dipping into the shot adds a nice touch.

10:08   Various ethnic music cues establish the many locations visited.

11:09   Exterior to interior environments are established with reverb.

14:22   The volume on the montage music is dipped momentarily for dialogue.

26:40   Foley footsteps

30:44   Futzed sound of 35 mm film is added to the shot to reinforce the archival footage.

38:00   Romantic music gets interrupted for comic effect. Subsequent audio is treated to imply bad production audio.

40:40   Feedback is added to the boom pole movement to make fun of the notion of production audio in animation.

52:57   Extended vari-speed effect to show how hard he is working.

TANGLED (2010) SOUND: CAMERON FRANKLEY,
SCORE: ALAN MENKEN

1:06:55   This scene is a musical duet with Rapunzel and Flynn Rider. The song is presented through their interior thoughts rather than lip sync. This design approach plays nicely on the notion that Rapunzel must not reveal her feelings or her location. By the end of the song, Rapunzel and Flynn are able to share their thoughts openly through song.

1:16:20   This cue builds as Rapunzel's true identity is revealed. Whooshes provided transitional sound for flashbacks and camera moves.

TARZAN (1999) SOUND: PER HALLBERG, SCORE: MARK MANCINA

00:00	Title sequence provides back-story. Sound and score accompany each form edit that transitions us between the world of the humans and the apes.
11:09	Source to underscore.
15:52	The sound of a race car exaggerates Tarzan's speedy pass by.
25:30	The cue builds toward a misdirection.
28:40	Tarzan's scream is seamlessly pitched with the underscore.
42:05	This sequence is a clever blending of SFX and score.
109:40	The elephant trunk is caricatured with a trumpet.

TITAN A.E. (2000) SOUND: MATTHEW WOOD, SCORE: GRAEME REVELL/TIM SIMONEC

38:13	Synthetic dialogue with subtitles.
42:30	Synthetic dialogue with subtitles.
51:45	Synthetic dialogue with subtitles.

TOY STORY I (1995) SOUND: TIM HOLLAND, SCORE: RANDY NEWMAN

09:13	Group ADR for children attending the birthday party, mostly off-screen.
11:17	Futzed radio
14:47	Buzz Lightyear breathing from inside his helmet. POV
18:56	Toy plane sound transitions to WW II dive bomber for exaggeration.
21:43	Pleasant BGs coming from Andy's window.
32:20	Dialogue enhancement as Buzz discusses his mission.
34:34	Toolbox crash post-laps with a ring-out.

35:20	The straw movements in a cup is used for footstep Foley.
39:00	The BGs for Sid's environment are consistent with his dark personality.
44:44	The sound of the dog's breathing is exaggerated, representing the toys' perspective.
45:55	The mockup Buzz Lightyear television commercial is futzed.
55:41	Wind-up clock sound is used to transition from Sid's room to Andy's room.
1:06:30	Woody's voice is futzed initially and then transitions to full resolution on the line "So Play Nice."
1:12:04	The tension in the shot is temporarily broken when we hear source music "Hakuna Matata" (cultural referent) from *The Lion King* futzed in the interior of the car.
1:14:59	Sleigh bells are introduced in the score as the shot pre-laps from summer to winter.

TOY STORY II (1999) SOUND: MICHAEL SILVERS, SCORE: RANDY NEWMAN

00:33	The entire opening sequence is a misdirection and homage to *Star Wars*.
04:26	Zurg's laugh transitions to a futzed version as video game play is revealed.
10:29	This extended dream sequence becomes very subjective at 11:08.
20:15	The BGs from Big Al's apartment include emergency vehicles to establish the danger that Woody is in.
27:58	The source music is treated with a vari-speed effect to reinforce the phonograph.
32:01	Buzz Lightyear's dialogue is enhanced with underscore, eventually morphing into the "Star Spangled Banner." This concept is continued as the underscore becomes source for a television sign off.

37:24   The cue plays only when the toys move.

58:20   The footsteps are represented by both music cue (sneak steps) and Foley.

1:10:42   Cheesy source music creates a comic relief while also establishing the space.

TREASURE PLANET (2002) SOUND: DANE DAVIS/ JULIA EVERSHADE, SCORE: JAMES NEWTON HOWARD

00:31   The implied narration sets up the misdirection which is soon revealed as diegetic (talking book). Vari-speed is applied to the sound track for both the closing and opening of the book.

06:07   Dialogue is treated with a Vocorder to create a robotic effect.

17:18   An alien speaks in "Flatula," no subtitles provided for interpretation.

33:07   John Silver's voice post-laps.

UP (2009) SOUND: TOM MYERS/MICHAEL SILVERS, SCORE: MICHAEL GIACCHINO

00:49   The opening sequence is futzed and sweetened with film warping sound. The soundtrack transitions from diegetic to non-diegetic, as the narrator becomes a product of Carl's imagination.

12:04   Exaggerated cracking sound to direct the audience's attention to Carl's bad back. This is followed by off-screen sound of electric stair chair. Both sounds are used to develop the character.

21:50   This sequence is an extended fantasy sequence with non-literal treatment as not to reveal the misdirection.

26:34   A radio squelch is added to Carl's hearing aid as he turns it down to avoid hearing Russell talk (POV).

50:08   The word "roof" as spoken by Dug is substituted with an actual bark that sounds similar.

VALIANT (2005) SOUND: DANNY SHEEHAN/ MATTHEW COLLINGE, SCORE: GEORGE FENTON

02:15   Futzed propaganda reel with period music. The cash register sound represents quality enlists and the Kalooga horn is used for the rejects.

06:24   The BGs and score are dark for scenes with the bad guys.

29:00   Dialogue enhancement.

45:06   The use of reverb to transition movements from the street to the sewer.

47:43   Source music.

WALL-E (2008) SOUND: BENN BURTT/MATTHEW WOOD, SCORE: THOMAS NEWMAN

00:00   Nearly 23 minutes go by without any principal dialogue yet the narrative is effectively communicated. This is an extraordinary accomplishment in sound design.

00:00   The title sequence is scored with "Put on your Sunday Clothes" from *Hello, Dolly!* This is an anempathetic choice of music that is treated with multiple perspectives to match each of the environments that Wall-E moves through.

05:05   The dialogue in the B & L commercial provides the back-story.

10:00   The Macintosh power up chord is used to represent Wall-E becoming fully recharged.

23:07   The first recognizable words by the principal characters Wall-E and Eve are digitally processed and faintly recognizable.

WALLACE AND GROMIT: THE CURSE OF THE WERE-RABBIT (2005) SOUND: JAMES MATHER, SCORE: JULIAN NOTT

02:45   The beeps for the eyes are used as a transitional device for the form edit that follows.

23:32   Car alarm is used to represent the securing of the greenhouse.

27:45   Underscore is revealed as source as a comic effect.

39:20	The ringing of the dog's eyes transition via a form edit to actual bells.
47:25	Cliché thunder claps for repeated dialogue and whooshed for camera move.
51:02	Music cue syncs each time the dog points his finger.

WHO FRAMED ROGER RABBIT (1988) SOUND: CHARLES CAMPBELL/LOUIS EDEMANN, SCORE: ALAN SILVESTRI

00:33	Homage to Carl Stalling and the early Warner Brothers cartoons.
09:01	Underscore to source.
22:13	Dialogue from Marvin Acme transitions to Roger Rabbit "Patty Cake." The sound is meant to make upsetting off-screen action implicit.
111:05	Isomorphic cue follows camera moves.
113:20	Foley footsteps transition to a train sound for exaggeration.

THE WILD (2006) SOUND: ANDY NEWELL, SCORE: ALAN SILVESTRI

00:00	Narration to on-screen dialogue. The underscore starts and stops with each story being told.
4:40	Whip Foley for squirrel Kung Fu followed by a cash register sound as the steak is delivered to Sampson.
11:08	Prepared piano as isomorphism.
36:30	The sound of a whip and horse whinny exaggerate the squirrels' pantomime of horseback riding.
37:00	The eye blink is covered with a camera shutter.
53:26	Echo.
58:56	Isomorphic cue for the camera zoom.
1:00:30	Sampson's instincts are represented by reverberant V.O.

THE WILD THORNBERRYS (2002) SOUND: BETH STERNER, SCORE: RANDY KERBER/DREW NEUMANN

30:41   The clock slows down and has reverb added, making it a transitional device to the dream sequence.

42:06   Underscore cadences and dialogue pre-laps with parachute wipe followed by futzed radio.

46:20   Ham radio split is futzed when voice is off-screen.

47:25   Elephant trumpet sound has a ring out to post-lap.

54:58   Cue fades in with visual wipe.

BIBLIOGRAPHY

SOUND THEORY

Alten, S., *Audio in Media*. New York: Wadsworth, 1998.

Altman, R., *Sound Theory Sound Practice*. New York: Routledge, 1992.

Cantine, J., *Shot by Shot*. Pittsburgh, PA: Pittsburgh Filmmakers, 2000.

Chion, M., *Audio-Vision: Sound on Screen*. New York: Columbia University Press, 1994.

Holman, T., *Sound for Film and Television*. Boston, MA: Focal Press, 1997.

Kenny, T., *Sound for Picture*. Vallego, CA: MixBooks, 1997.

Lack, R., *Twenty Four Frames Under*. London: Interlink Books, 1999.

LoBrutto, V., *Sound on Film: Interviews with Creators of Film Sound*. Westport, CT: Praeger, 1994.

Murch, W., *In the Blink of an Eye: A Perspective on Film Editing*. 2nd Ed. Los Angeles: Silman-James Press, 2001.

Sider, L., *Soundscape: The School of Sound Lectures*. New York: Wallflower Press, 2003.

Sonnenschein, D., *Sound Design: The Expressive Power of Music, Voice, and Sound Effects in Cinema*. Studio City, CA: Michael Wiese Productions, 2001.

Thom, R., *Designing A Movie for Sound*. Sweden: FilmSound.org, 1999.

Thompson, R., *Grammar of the Edit*. New York, NY: Focal Press, 2005.

Thompson, R., *Grammar of the Shot*. New York, NY: Focal Press, 2005.

SOUND TECHNIQUES

Adam, T., *The Best Effect Settings for Sound Design and Mixing*. Bremen, Germany: Wizoo GmbH, 2000.

Ament, V., *The Foley Grail: The Art of Performing Sound to Film*. New York, NY: Focal Press, 2009.

Apple Computers Inc, *Mastered for iTunes: Music as the Artist and Sound Engineer Intended*, January, 2012.

Bell, D., *Getting the Best Score for Your Film*. Beverly Hills, CA: Silman-James Press, 1994.

Berg, R., *The Physics of Sound*, 2nd edn. New York: Simon & Schuster, 1994.

Churchill, S., *The Indie Guide to Music Supervision*. Los Angeles, CA: Filmic Press, 2000.

Collins, M., *Audio Plug-Ins and Virtual Instruments*. Boston, MA: Focal Press, 2003.

Collins, M., *Choosing and Using Audio and Music Software*. Boston, MA: Focal Press, 2004.

Eargle, J., *The Microphone Book*. Boston, MA: Focal Press, 2001.

Gibson, D., *The Art of Mixing*. Vallego, CA: Mix Books, 1997.

Huber, D., *Modern Recording Techniques*. Boston, MA: Focal Press, 2001.

Jackson, B., *Shark Tale*: A different kind of fish story. *Mix Magazine*, Sept. 2004.

Katz, B., *Mastering Audio: The Art and the Science*. Boston, MA: Focal Press, 2002.

Kerner, M., *The Art of the Sound Effects Editor*. Boston, MA: Focal Press, 1989.

Lehrman, P. and Tully, T., *MIDI for the Professional*. New York: Amsco, 1993.

Lott, R., *Sound Effects: Radio, TV, and Film*. Boston, MA: Focal Press, 1990.

Lustig, M., *Music Editing for Motion Pictures*. New York: Hasting House, 1980.

Moravcsik, M., *Musical Sound: An Introduction to the Physics of Music*, St. Paul, MN: Paragon House, 2002.

Moulton, D., *Audio Lecture Series*, Vols. 1–4. Boulder, CO: Music Maker, 2000.

Moulton, D., *Total Recording*. Sherman Oaks, CA: KIQ Productions, 2000.

Northam, M. and Miller, L., *Film and Television Composers Resource Guide*. Milwaukee, WI: Hal Leonard, 1998.

Purcell, J., *Dialogue Editing for Motion Pictures*. Boston, MA: Focal Press, 2007.

Rose, J., *Producing Great Sound for Digital Video*. San Francisco, CA: CMP Books, 1999.

Rose, J., *Audio Postproduction for Digital Video*. San Francisco, CA: CMP Books, 2002.

Rossing, T., *The Science of Sound*, 3rd edn. Boston, MA: Addison-Wesley, 2001.

Shepherd, A., *Pro Tools for Video, Film, and Multimedia*. Boston, MA: Muska and Lipman, 2003.

Smith, M., *Broadcast Sound Technology*. Boston, MA: Butterworth, 1990.

White, G., *Audio Dictionary*. Seattle, WA: University of Washington Press, 1991.

LEGAL REFERENCE MATERIAL

Donaldson, M., *Clearance and Copyright*. Los Angeles, CA: Silman-James Press, 1996.

Miller, P., *Media Law for Producers*. Boston, MA: Focal Press, 2003.

Stim, R., *Getting Permission: How To License and Clear Copyrighted Material Online and Off*. Berkeley, CA: Nolo Press, 2001.

ANIMATION SOUND HISTORY

Goldmark, D. and Taylor, Y., *The Cartoon Music Book*. Chicago, IL: A Cappella Books, 2002.

Lawson, T. and Persons, A., *The Magic Behind the Voices*. Jackson, MS: University Press of Mississippi, 2004

Maltin, L., *Of Mice and Magic: A History of American Animated Cartoons.* New York: New American Library, 1987.

ANIMATION TECHNIQUE

Arijon, D., *Grammar of the Film Language*, Los Angeles, CA: Silman-James Press, 1976.

Blair, P., *Cartoon Animation.* Laguna Hills, CA: Walter Foster, 1995.

Culhane, S., *Animation: From Script to Screen.* New York: St. Martin's Press, 1988.

Kozloff, S., *Invisible Storytellers: Voice-Over Narration in American Fiction Film.* Berkeley: University of California Press, 1989.

Osipa, J., *Stop Staring: Facial Animation Done Right.* Alameda, CA: Sybex, 2003.

Simon, M., *Producing Independent 2D Animation.* Boston, MA: Focal Press, 2003.

Whitaker, H., *Timing for Animation.* Boston, MA: Focal Press, 1981.

Williams, R., *Animators Survival Kit.* New York: Faber & Faber, 2002.

Winder, C. and Dowlatabadi, Z., *Producing Animation.* Boston, MA: Focal Press, 2001.

REFERENCE BOOKS

Breeze, C., *Digital Audio Dictionary.* Indianapolis, IN: Howard W. Sams, 1999.

Konigsberg, I., *The Complete Film Dictionary.* New York: Penguin Group, 1987.

ARTICLES

Benzuly, S., Production music libraries in 2004. *Mix Magazine*, April 1, 2004.

Droney, M., Avast and away! *Mix Magazine*, Jan. 1, 2003.

Hawkins, E., Cartoon cutups: music editing for TV animation. *Electronic Musician*, June 1, 2000.

O, S., Build a personal studio on any budget, Part I. *Electronic Musician*, July 1, 2002.

Peck, N., Sound by design. *Electronic Musician*, March 1, 2001.

Peck, N., Making the cut. *Electronic Musician*, June 1, 2004.

Robair, G., Build a personal studio an any budget, Part II. *Electronic Musician*, July 1, 2002.

PRODUCTION FEATURETTES

A Guy Like You: Multi-Language Reel, *Hunchback of Notre Dame*, Walt Disney Pictures, 1996.

Anastasia: A Magical Journey, *Anastasia*, 20th Century Fox, 1997.

Creating the Voice of "Casey Jr.," *Dumbo*, Walt Disney Pictures, 1941.

Films Are Not Released; They Escape, S*tar Wars II: Attack of the Clones*, 20th Century Fox, 2002.

Jimmy Neutron: Boy Genius, Paramount, 2001.

Looney Tunes: Golden Collection, Warner Brothers Pictures, 2000.

Music and Sound Design, *Dinosaur*, Walt Disney Pictures, 2000.

You're Not Elected, Charlie Brown, *It's a Great Pumpkin, Charlie Brown*, Paramount Pictures, 1966.

70/30 Law, *Treasure Planet*, Walt Disney Pictures, 2002.

Supplemental Features, *Toy Story*, Pixar, 1999.

The Making of Jurassic Park, *Jurassic Park Collector's Edition*, Universal Pictures, 2000.

Walt Disney Treasures: Silly Symphonies, Vol. 4, Walt Disney Pictures, 1991.

INDEX

Note: Page numbers in *italics* are for tables, those in **bold** are for figures.

Printed and bound by CPI Group (UK) Ltd, Croydon, CR0 4YY

22/10/2024

01777635-0003